_8_

WITHDRAWN

BY JOSEPH BRODSKY

Elegy for John Donne and Other Poems

Selected Poems

A Part of Speech

Less Than One

To Urania

Marbles

MARBLES

JOSEPH BRODSKY

MARBLES

A PLAY IN THREE ACTS

TRANSLATED BY ALAN MYERS

WITH THE AUTHOR

FARRAR / STRAUS / GIROUX

NEW YORK

Library of Congress Cataloging-in-Publication Data
Brodsky, Joseph.
[Mramor. English]
Marbles: a play in three acts / Joseph Brodsky;
translated by Alan Myers, with the author.—1st ed.
Translation of: Mramor.
I. Title.
PG3479.4.R64M713   1989   891.72'44—dc19   88–21188

MARBLES

A C T I

The second century after our era.

The prison cell of P U B L I U S *and* T U L L I U S : *an ideal enclosure for two, a cross between a bachelor pad and the cabin of
a spacecraft. The decor is more Palladio than Piranesi. The view
from the window must convey an impression of considerable altitude (clouds drifting by, say), since the prison is located in a
gigantic steel tower, approximately one mile high. The window
can either be round, like a porthole, or have rounded corners,
like a TV screen.*

*In the center of the cell is a column in the Doric style con-
taining an elevator. This column passes through the entire
tower and is, in fact, a pivot (or a piston): everything that
appears on stage and disappears from it in the course of the play
does so through the shaft's opening, which is a combination
of a dumbwaiter and a rubbish chute. Alongside this opening
there is the door of the main elevator, which opens only once—at
the beginning of Act III.*

On either side of the shaft are the alcoves of P U B L I U S *and*
T U L L I U S. *All modern conveniences: bath, table, washbasin,
lavatory, telephone, TV set fixed into the wall, bookshelves. On
these and in niches in the wall are busts of classics.*

It is midday.

P U B L I U S , *a man of thirty to thirty-five, stout, balding, is
listening to a canary singing in its cage, which stands on the
windowsill. After the curtain rises, a minute passes during which
nothing can be heard save the canary singing.*

P U B L I U S : Ah, Tullius! As the poet says, what must the Almighty hear up there in Paradise, if here on earth such sounds
caress our ears.

(T U L L I U S, *about ten years senior to* P U B L I U S, *lean and wiry, hair fairish. As the curtain goes up, he is reclining in a steaming bath, reading and smoking*)

T U L L I U S *(Without looking up from the book)*: What poet?
P U B L I U S: I forget. A Persian, I think.
T U L L I U S: Barbarian. *(Turns a page)*
P U B L I U S: Well, what if he is.
T U L L I U S: Barbarian. Them savages. Dark ass. Mutton guzzlers.

(Pause; the canary singing)

P U B L I U S *(Imitates the bird)*: Uli-ti-ti-tyu-tyu-uuu-u . . .

(T U L L I U S turns the tap on harder; sound of rushing water)

P U B L I U S: U-li-ti-ti-tyu-yu-u-u-uuu . . . Tullius!
T U L L I U S: What?
P U B L I U S: Have you got any of that gâteau left?
T U L L I U S: Look in the bedside cupboard . . . Scoffed your own down by now, have you . . . Animal lover.
P U B L I U S: It was pure accident, Tullius, you realize. I didn't mean to. It's just that the gâteau was so unexpected. That's why I couldn't mean to. Actually, I wanted to leave it. Well, that was afterward, when I'd eaten it . . . You see, it was so sudden! All my time inside, I've never set eyes on a gâteau.
T U L L I U S: And you won't again, either. Not this one, anyway.
P U B L I U S: Oh? Why?
T U L L I U S: Read the rules. *(Throws his book on the floor, stretches in the bath)* They've got a computer down there. Which composes the menus. "Repetition of dishes is possible once every two hundred and forty-three years." Unquote.

PUBLIUS: How come you know that?

TULLIUS: Like I said: Read the rules. It's all there. Volume VI, page 30. Letter *N*—Nutrition . . . You'd better familiarize yourself.

PUBLIUS: I am not a masochist.

TULLIUS: Well, masochist or not, my sweet Publius, you won't see gâteaux ever again. To the end of your days. Unless you are the Wandering Jew, of course.

PUBLIUS: Unfortunately not. Wait, what am I saying! Blissfully not.

TULLIUS: Scratch in the cupboard anyway. Poor canary . . .

*(*PUBLIUS *makes for* TULLIUS*'s alcove, opens the bedside cupboard, and rummages about in it; he extracts a piece of gâteau, looks at it for some time, then suddenly eats it all up with unexpected speed)*

TULLIUS *(Shouts indignantly, climbing out of the bath)*: What d'you think you are doing, you bastard! That was for the canary! *(Abruptly calms down)* Oh well. *(Climbs back into the bath)* It's always the same story. First you starve the kitten to death. Then the goldfish. Then that bunny rabbit. Now, I see, you're taking on the canary . . .

PUBLIUS *(Agitated)*: That's not so, Tullius. I didn't mean . . .

TULLIUS *(Raising himself on his elbows)*: And didn't it cross your mind that the bird most likely had never even seen a gâteau before?

PUBLIUS *(Completely crushed, wanders over to the window, taps on the cage with his finger)*: Uli-ti-ti-tyu-uuuu-u-u . . . *(The canary remains silent)* Uli-ti-ti-tyuuuuu-u-u . . . And now what, eh? Have to wait till dinnertime, eh? *(Talks to himself)* Although dinner, come to think . . . They've always got something lined up . . . fancy stuff . . . to keep the bowels moving . . . never had any bother going . . . it's so we live longer . . . all my time inside, never once been constipated . . . Yeah, those computers . . . Let you go then, shall we? *(Pause)* Tullius!

T U L L I U S : What now?

P U B L I U S : Shall we let it go, then, eh?

T U L L I U S : Yes, let's.

P U B L I U S : On the other hand, though, it *does* sing.

T U L L I U S : Bugger off!

(Pause; P U B L I U S *goes over to the telephone, picks up the receiver, and dials a number)*

P U B L I U S : Mr. Praetor, sir. This is Publius Marcellus in 1750. Well, you see, I have this little bird here. Yes, a canary. Exactly. There isn't any chance of having some millet or hemp seed, is there? Yes, yes, millet's best. Wha-a-a-t? Will be included in my ration weight? You mean, the main course will be a hundred grams less? But really . . . Ah, I see-e. Yes. I withdraw my request. *(Drops the receiver)* Damn it!

T U L L I U S : What's the matter?

P U B L I U S : Bloody lift! . . . They claim it operates on a fixed program. Says my main course will be reduced by half. Praetor. Creep.

T U L L I U S : And what's the main course today?

P U B L I U S *(Pressing the button in the bed head and quickly glancing at the message on the screen)*: Cockscombs. Sautéed.

T U L L I U S : What with?

P U B L I U S : Horseradish.

T U L L I U S : Mm—yes.

P U B L I U S : Once in a lifetime.

T U L L I U S : Sadists, no question about it.

P U B L I U S : Specially the Praetor.

T U L L I U S : The Praetor's got nothing to do with it. It's the elevator that's the trouble. Down goes the crap, up comes the grub. Strictly in proportion. *Perpetuum mobile* . . . All I'd like to know is which came first.

PUBLIUS: Meaning?

TULLIUS: Which came first—the chicken or the egg?

PUBLIUS: That's exactly what I'll ask the Almighty. On the Day of Judgment.

TULLIUS: Barbarian. I meant the menu.

PUBLIUS: I was only kidding.

TULLIUS: Barbarian all the same. All the faithful are. Even the doubting ones. Give me the phone.

PUBLIUS: Be my guest. *(Passes the telephone over to* TULLIUS*)*

TULLIUS: Hello. Mr. Praetor, sir. This is Tullius Varro in 1750. Why have you put a barbarian in my cell? He believes in God. Or rather, he doesn't. But all the same in God. What was the committee doing? This man isn't a Roman. Yes, there has been a mistake. No, no more complaints. Ah, that's what you think! Mr. Praetor, you are a shit. I shall complain to the Senate. Yes, I'll find a way. *(Puts the receiver down)*

PUBLIUS: What did he say?

TULLIUS: Nothing to be done, he says. Creed, he says, is no criterion. Nor is its absence.

PUBLIUS: What *is* the criterion?

TULLIUS: Physical presence, says he, within the imperial boundaries, plus the absence of any alternative. That is, when there is nowhere else to turn. Which, he says, according to the last decree, applies to all mammals.

PUBLIUS: I told you, he is a bastard.

TULLIUS: No, Praetor's got nothing to do with it. It's all Caligula's doing. He thinks that because he is the namesake, he has a right . . . Plus the committees have all gone completely to seed. Speaking of mammals, they've put a horse on the Senate civil-rights commission: Secretatus is the name. From Secretariat and Citation. And Citation itself was Incitatus' foal, mind you. Well, I don't object: our Senate has always been the most representative. Throughout all human history. Someone, after all, has to defend the animals' interests. And given his pedigree, especially his Secretariat connection, Secretatus seems the ideal choice . . . But civil rights! Secretatus is putting it about now that the computer center databank, the one set up under Tiberius, is out of date.

PUBLIUS: That is?

TULLIUS: That is, that is! That is, it has been established that in all ages, under the Pharaohs, in Greece, Rome, during Christianity, among Muslims and the slant-eyed—well, you name it—in all ages, approximately 6.7 percent of the population was kept under lock and key. It's true, though, that in later Christianity the percentage was something like three times higher. But if you spread this business out over all human history, it boils down to about 6.7 percent for each generation.

PUBLIUS: Well, it's not exactly a hell of a lot . . .

TULLIUS: Just as many as necessary . . . And on the basis of these data, Tiberius fixed, once and for all, the number of prisoners in these parts. That's genuine judicial reform, right! Yes, but Tiberius went still further. He reduced the 6.7 percent to 3 percent. Because in those days there were all sorts of terms in operation. Under the Christians, for instance, a ten-year stretch was popular; so was a twenty-fiver. Anyway, Tiberius took the arithmetical mean and, having abolished capital punishment, put out a decree by which we . . .

PUBLIUS: That is, the 3 percent?

TULLIUS: Yes, by which the 3 percent got to do life. Whether you've committed a crime or not. A kind of tax. The Senate, naturally, supported him, and the civil-rights commission set up a committee to see that the arrests were randomized. And now this Secretatus is stirring it and insisting on a review of the databank.

PUBLIUS: But in what way?

TULLIUS: No idea; just neighs . . . *(Imitates horse neighing)* Ihahahacivil . . . Ihahaharights . . . *(Pause)* They've got those electronic interpreters there. Space programs' spin-offs. Damn them all.

PUBLIUS: But what's his view—that the percentage should be higher? or lower?

TULLIUS: Beats me. Lower, most likely. Playing the liberal.

PUBLIUS: Well, that's all right, then.

TULLIUS *(Shouting)*: And just what's good about it?! Just what is so hot about it?

PUBLIUS: Well, how can I put it . . . It'll get more spacious around here anyway . . . They'd cram all sorts of garbage in otherwise . . .

TULLIUS: But it's garbage just the same! And who needs space in a cell! Just use your brains: space, in a cell. Don't mix it up with a private apartment.

PUBLIUS *(Pensively)*: There's nothing easier: to convert an apartment into a cell. Or a cell into an apartment.

TULLIUS: Precisely!

PUBLIUS: Now, now, Tullius . . . simmer down . . . The Senate is not likely to take it up.

TULLIUS *(Gloomily)*: You never know. After all, he fought in Libya. Services. Besides, they're all of them nuts about liberals . . . And as for Caligula, he just pisses boiled water when he hears his mare speechifying.

PUBLIUS: Say it again? Who boils it? He or his horse?

TULLIUS: Doesn't matter. Where is my toga?

PUBLIUS: Over there, where you dumped it. *(Points toward* TULLIUS*'s alcove)* If you are through, don't let the water out.

TULLIUS: Barbarian. Insane about economizing. ,

PUBLIUS *(Starts to undress)*: Well, if I economize on anything, it's only time`. . . As for insanity, all Rome isn't exactly *in corpore sano* when it comes to its water supply. Rather, *in corpore sauna.* You think I can't see through it, right? The Tiber would have gone dry years ago had we been using it. What's grand about the water supply in these parts is that the level in the pipes is permanent! Irrespective of the Tiber! Physics! Connecting vessels! It's all to do with the filter system! *(Climbs into the bath with* TULLIUS*)* As the poet says, "There is no way to step twice into the same stream." Rubbish. One most certainly can. *(Luxuriating)* Ah-a-a . . . Aqua . . . H_2O . . . See: neither more nor less . . . except when it evaporates . . . or else when you dry yourself . . . hardly even then . . . 'cause eventually the towel goes to the wash and gives back what's been absorbed anyway . . . I am pretty sure that this tower of ours is also a water tower.

TULLIUS: That's what they say.

PUBLIUS: And I am convinced that someone—somewhere— has already washed in this water. It has a whiff of something . . . well, not exactly native, but familiar.

TULLIUS: Could be that Caligula washed in it.

PUBLIUS: And Tiberius.

TULLIUS: And Secretatus . . .

PUBLIUS: If only filters could talk . . . *(Pause)* And my wife washed in it . . . and yours . . .

TULLIUS *(Sharply)*: And what do you mean by that?

PUBLIUS: No, no, nothing like that . . . And the kids, too. Once water, always water, after all. Whether it's an apartment or a cell. Like I said: connecting vessels.

TULLIUS: Connecting for some. For others they ain't . . . Besides, look! you're spilling it!

PUBLIUS: Big deal. Big farting deal.

TULLIUS *(Indignantly; rising out of the bath)*: You are

diminishing the Tiber! Not to mention messing up filters! *(Abruptly calms down)* I mean, that's what causes forgetfulness. Lacunae is the word. Assault on the public memory. A crime against history . . . Against the cause-and-effect principle, that is. For *aqua conservut omnia.*

PUBLIUS: Big farting deal . . . Who cares for aqua anyhow? Who cares for cause-and-effect anyway? *(Pause)* Especially for effect . . .

(Pause)

PUBLIUS: It's so odd, Tullius, isn't it. I mean, I knew that sort of thing might happen. Even as a child I did. We all know. All the more so because my father was never arrested. Nor granddad. Yet somehow I just couldn't imagine. Got myself a family, kids . . .

TULLIUS: Now, now, Publius . . . It only shows that our committee is doing a really fine job.

PUBLIUS *(Somewhat astonished)*: How do you make that out?

TULLIUS: Because they put you in only after you've reproduced. Just about when you're getting sick of the wife, etc. When just about everything ceases to make sense. When the expression "for life" begins to mean something. Not earlier . . . The computer, remember . . .

PUBLIUS: Yeah . . . Technology . . . *(Pause)* What's that you're reading?

TULLIUS: Horace.

PUBLIUS: And how is it?

TULLIUS: A classic. A bit overenthusiastic perhaps. Like all oldsters. That *aqua conservut omnia* business . . . It's his.

PUBLIUS: Maybe we should order a bust of him.

TULLIUS: Especially as there is no need to feed it.

PUBLIUS: And what about the canary?

TULLIUS: Let it go. Otherwise it'll die of hunger. Or the rarefied air.

PUBLIUS: Pity.

TULLIUS: To let it go, or that it'll die?

PUBLIUS: Both. To let it go as well. It'll fly, you know, in all four . . . In all 360 degrees, that is . . . Needless thoughts, you know . . . 'Cause we're the ones stuck here, aren't we . . . Till the end of our days . . . Nobody will let *us* out, mind you. For us, this *is* life. Meaning. Why her, then? Why let her out?

TULLIUS: She'll snuff it otherwise.

PUBLIUS: And won't we? We, Tullius, we'll snuff it, too. Who'll pity us, eh? She maybe? What with? Hasn't got any brains, like I said . . . And even if she had, it wouldn't amount to much. Wouldn't cover both of us anyway.

TULLIUS: I take it you don't believe in miniaturization.

PUBLIUS: That's not the point . . . Whereas we can be sorry for her. And on top of that, she sings.

(Pause)

TULLIUS: I'll feel sorry for you when you snuff it. If, as you think, the scale is all that matters.

PUBLIUS *(Embraces* TULLIUS*)*: Be sorry for me now, Tullius.

TULLIUS: Get your paws off.

PUBLIUS: Better be sorry for me now, eh . . .

TULLIUS: Take your hands off, do you hear!

PUBLIUS: But I didn't mean anything . . .

TULLIUS: No? And whose member is this, then? You've got an erection. *(Climbs out of the bath)* Where's my toga?

PUBLIUS *(Settling himself more comfortably in the bath)*: So much for fine words. "I'll be sorry . . ." Indeed! I know how sorry you are going to be. Me, I'll go down the chute, and some imbecile will grace my place. I'm down, he's up.

TULLIUS: That's but the way the lift functions. The balance principle. Symbol of justice.

P U B L I U S (*Continuing in the same tone*): You'll be prattling
with him, this and that . . . Maybe even, well—rubbing shoul-
ders—if he's young, that is . . . Main thing . . . the main thing
is, it's bound to be some sort of idiot . . . garbage, like you
said . . . a shepherd boy, or a lictor. But you won't remember
me, oh no. Out of sight, out of mind . . . Change the sheets, so
to speak . . .

T U L L I U S : Precisely.

P U B L I U S : Sure. No fuss, that's best. Instinct for self-preserva-
tion, plus the airs of a stoic. One and the same thing, in any
case. With full support from the Praetor, of course. And just
when you've got yourself completely preserved, they tip you
down the chute as well.

(Pause)

T U L L I U S (*Wrapping himself in his toga*): Such is the common lot.

P U B L I U S : Yeah, sure. You're above all that.

T U L L I U S : The main thing is to maintain the percentage.

P U B L I U S : A citizen. A pillar of the state. *(Pause)* Dog shit.

T U L L I U S : Barbarian. Maybe even a Christian. Scared of
death. What sort of Roman are you! Family, kids . . . arsehole.
All that's barbarism. A yearning for freedom! What do you
know about freedom? Broads, that's all. Were you given a
choice between pumping a hetaera and just rotting on your
cot, which would you choose?

P U B L I U S : The hetaera, of course.

T U L L I U S : There you are! For you there's a difference.
Whereas there is none, Publius. There is no difference whatsoever. For the days go by. That's all there is to it, that the days
go by. No matter what you think you're doing, you stand still,
but the days go by. The main thing is time. Thus we were
taught by Tiberius. Rome's task is to merge with time. That's

life's meaning. To get rid of sentiments. Of all these la-di-das about women, kids, love, hate. To get rid of these ideas about freedom. And then you'll merge with time. For there will be nothing else but time. And after that you needn't even stir— you'll be going along with it. Without lagging behind or running ahead. You, yourself, are the clock. And not the one who's gazing at it. That's what we Romans believe in. Not to depend on time, that's freedom. While you are a barbarian, Publius, a dirty barbarian. And I'd have killed you if I hadn't known that they'd just replace you with another one, probably worse. From a more barbarian province. Especially now, when the committee is blessed with Secretatus.

P U B L I U S *(Turning onto his side in the bath)*: In that case . . . well, maybe I'll just do away with myself, eh? In the Roman fashion, right here, in the bath. Like Sulla.

T U L L I U S: They'll send a replacement all the same. *(Pause)* The lift, you know . . .

P U B L I U S: Good grief.

(Pause)

T U L L I U S: As the poet has it, "Alas, my beloved Postumus/ The fugitive years pass by."

P U B L I U S: Who said that?

T U L L I U S: Horace.

P U B L I U S: Good grief. *(Pause)* Give me that telephone.

T U L L I U S: Certainly.

P U B L I U S: Mr. Praetor, sir. This is Publius Marcellus in 1750. Would you be good enough to send a bust of the poet Horace to our cell. Yes, Horace. *(Aside to* T U L L I U S*)* Spell it . . .

T U L L I U S: Homer, Ovid, Ramses, Achilles . . .

P U B L I U S: Homer, Ovid, Ramses, Achilles.

T U L L I U S: Caesar, Ennius . . .

P U B L I U S: Caesar, Ennius. Yes, Quintus Horatius Flaccus.

What do you mean, will it take up a lot of space? What's the difference, Mr. Praetor? Yes, prison is a shortage of space compensated by a surplus of time . . . Yes, the sooner the better. What goes down?

TULLIUS: The chessmen. With the board.

PUBLIUS: The chessmen go down . . . Much obliged, Mr. Praetor. *(Puts down receiver)* Bastard, that praetor. Ignoramus.

TULLIUS: Good job, though.

PUBLIUS: Why?

TULLIUS: Well, chatting on the phone. All he's got to do.

PUBLIUS: Mm—yes. A thousand sesterces. Everything's government issue. Nothing to worry about. Just procreate and keep an eye on the computer. What a fool I was not to apply when they announced a vacancy.

TULLIUS: They wouldn't hire you anyway.

PUBLIUS: Why's that?

TULLIUS: Nobody was ever arrested in your family. That sort of person can't be employed by the government. On the whole one gets to be a praetor, senator, consul only if one's ancestors did time in the Tower. Even at fourth remove. What good would an official be to Rome if one fine day . . . Just think, what sort of a senator can you make if your prospect is the Tower?

PUBLIUS: Well, true enough.

TULLIUS: One consolation is that the children will make it. Or grandchildren. For four generations minimum. *(Pause)* What's your kid called?

PUBLIUS: Octavian.

TULLIUS: Got a nice ring to it . . . He'll easily make a praetor. Or a senator. Maybe even a consul. Perhaps, who knows, even a princeps. A fine name is a ticket to success. Half the battle. It was smart of Tiberius to abolish church names. What kind of princeps would a Nikita make? Or worse still—Stanley? Even children would giggle. While Octavian, that's really something! It's as good as Tiberius. I called my oldest Tiberius.

P U B L I U S : And what about the youngest?

T U L L I U S : Also Tiberius. And the middle one . . .

P U B L I U S *(Pensively)*: Yeah . . . no matter what, he was a big man . . . Where would we all be if he hadn't thought up the Empire . . .

T U L L I U S : . . . and renamed the capital Rome . . . We'd just be rotting away, bit by bit . . . The backwoods of Europe.

P U B L I U S : Well, that's already something . . . *(Pause)* What's the weather like?

T U L L I U S *(Goes over to the window, looks down)*: Low, overcast. Can't see a damn thing. Clouds . . . Who knows, in Rome, maybe it's raining . . .

P U B L I U S : How's the thermometer?

T U L L I U S *(Without changing the pose)*: Ours or the one outside?

P U B L I U S : Outside.

T U L L I U S : Plus ten centigrade.

P U B L I U S : On the cool side.

T U L L I U S : What does it matter to you? Anyway, the thing's outside.

P U B L I U S : What of it? It's still a thermometer, isn't it? *(Pause)* Can't be raining in Rome, can it?

T U L L I U S : What's it to you?

P U B L I U S : I am a Roman . . . If only because I am here.

(Pause)

T U L L I U S : We're all Romans now. *(Glances at the thermometer)* Why on earth did they hang it there? Sadists.

P U B L I U S : When I was in the army, in Gaul, they brought a brothel to the cohort one day. And do you know what that bitch, that madame of theirs, thought up? She attached meters to the mattresses. Can you imagine?

TULLIUS: Still on about broads, aren't you? . . .

PUBLIUS: No, it's not that. I just recalled one legionary: the guy got short of cash . . . Real hunk of a man. Well, he had an ugly squint then, just like you now. An exact replica.

TULLIUS: Look at yourself, eyesore. *(Takes a book from the shelf and collapses on the bed)*

PUBLIUS *(Calculating out loud)*: Plus ten. Altitude—about half a mile above sea level. That's if you don't count Capitol Hill. With it, I guess, we'll make a mile almost, no less. Two-thirds of a mile then equals plus ten. In Rome in that case it must be some five degrees warmer. So if it's raining there, the rain's kind of warmish. The water in the Tiber, too, is muddy. Just as the poet says. People are bustling about. Cats in the windows are meowing. The Tower can't be seen. When it's raining nobody thinks about the Tower . . . Some architecture for you . . . I'd stroll to the Senate though. It's marvelous to sit in the Senate while it rains, listen to laws being debated. To vote . . . I, of course, would be "for the motion," whatever it was. And somebody would be against. What of it. That's what democracy's for. I guess I am a positivist by nature. And when the hands go up a sort of smell-wave passes through the entire hall. Armpits, perhaps . . . It's even more pleasant, as a matter of fact, when you vote with the minority . . . Eh, just think of it: sit all by yourself in the Senate—outside it's raining—it's kind of warm there—you put your hand up . . . *(Pause; raises his hand, sniffs)* . . . democracy . . . Tullius!

TULLIUS: Leave me alone.

PUBLIUS *(Resentfully)*: Avid reader, eh . . . so keen on the past . . . Sure, with all that history, who gives a damn about the present. Not to mention the future. Even about geography: not a scrap of it is left either. Just colonies: bits of Empire. Wherever you spit. Even if they've got independence . . . Nothing's left anymore but topography . . . Down—up . . . Go on, read . . . All of them. They'll stay on the shelf as you go down the chute . . . yes, sir . . . As the poet has it, *Dulce et decorum est pro patria mori* . . . Yes, *dulce* . . .

T U L L I U S : Which reminds me: what do we have today for dessert?

P U B L I U S : Wish it was gâteau again . . .

T U L L I U S : There are no agains here, I told you.

P U B L I U S : Yea-ah . . . everything repeats, save the menu.

T U L L I U S : You'd rather have it the other way around, eh?

P U B L I U S : Sure thing!

T U L L I U S : As I said: barbarian. *(Slams his book shut and rises)*

P U B L I U S : What's all this about barbarians! Would you quit yapping at me! Barbarian, barbarian. Like a dog barking . . .

T U L L I U S *(Sternly)*: A true Roman doesn't crave variety. To the true Roman it's all the same. The true Roman yearns for unity. And in that sense this menu of ours with all its specialties is a grave blunder. The menu should be permanent. Like the days. Like time itself. It's an oversight, our grub, I mean . . . The unity is not yet there . . . But it's coming . . .

P U B L I U S : What do you mean, all the same?! Equating a gâteau to its absence!

T U L L I U S : Yep. Since absence equals presence anyway. *Sub specie aeternitatis*, that is. That is, a true Roman considers differences sissy. So the menu's better if fixed.

P U B L I U S : There aren't going to be enough gâteaux for that. Neither will their absence do . . . Yeah . . . *dulce et decorum* . . .

T U L L I U S : Noble and sweet . . . Yet all the same it's coming. The unity, that is. I mean, of style. Nothing superfluous. Starting, technically speaking, with us.

P U B L I U S : Oh yes? So who was sorry for the canary?

T U L L I U S : Not sorry. Just some leftovers . . .

P U B L I U S : Well, same thing.

T U L L I U S : On the contrary. *(Pensively)* And yet it's a pity that it's a canary, and not, for instance, a wasp.

P U B L I U S : Wasp! What wasp?!

T u l l i u s: Because—miniaturization. Reduction to formula. A hieroglyph. A sign. Those computers' bits . . . how d'you call them? You know, when everything's a brain. The smaller the better. Of silicon . . .

P u b l i u s: Tullius!

T u l l i u s: Like the ancients had! . . . Chips! *(Cools off)* Well, what I mean is that if you had a wasp and caught it in a glass, and covered it with a saucer . . .

P u b l i u s: So?

T u l l i u s: So it's like a gladiator in the circus. Only without oxygen. Which alone smells of antiquity . . . And that glass, it's like a Colosseum, only miniaturized. Especially if it's not cut glass.

P u b l i u s: Well, so what?

T u l l i u s: So the canary is just too big. Almost an animal. The style's no good. Doesn't fit the age. Takes up a lot of space.

P u b l i u s: It ain't space, really. Just a cage.

T u l l i u s: Tautology, Publius. Tautology. There'd be more room for you, in the first place.

P u b l i u s: Well, you'll have a long wait for a wasp in here. And besides, they sting.

T u l l i u s: That's more honest than chirping. Under the circumstances. Anyway, it has stopped flying. It's stuffed itself too fat.

P u b l i u s *(Feeling his stomach)*: Yeah, a hundred-gram increase for a bird, it's not the same as for our ilk . . . Those maybe were my very considerations . . . when that gâteau . . .

T u l l i u s: Right. To say the least, your flying days are over.

P u b l i u s: The only consolation: I won't slide down that chute easily. With me, Tullius *(feels his waistline)*, you'll get a bag of trouble. You'll have plenty to be sorry for when I expire.

T u l l i u s: They've got a shredder there, Publius. A crushing knife. A cross between a mincing machine and the Tarpeian rock. As the decree puts it. I remember reading the decree . . .

when I was a kid, I think . . . Otherwise, people would be escaping . . . And after the shredder, the crocodiles . . .

P U B L I U S : I, too, remember reading that, in the old days, when
they still allowed visits, some used to sew in little balls under
the foreskin . . . to increase the diameter. Since the diameter is
what matters, not the length . . . Because broads, while you are
inside, fool around, right? And hence the idea that during the
visit she gets such . . . that she won't be able even to think of
anyone else. Only about you. And hence the balls. The pearl
ones are best, so they say. Although, come to think of it, where
could they get hold of mother-of-pearl over there? . . . Wrong
latitudes . . . Or the ones made of ebonite—the stuff they used
to make styluses of in those days . . . You'd file yourself a couple
of little balls, two to three millimeters in diameter, right,
polish them carefully—and then march to the *cocktor*. And this
cocktor would insert them under the skin. Under the foreskin,
that is . . . You'd wrap it up in a dock leaf for a couple of days—
and off to the rendezvous . . . Some wouldn't have them taken
out even when they were released. Just refused.

T U L L I U S : That's why Tiberius abolished visits . . .

P U B L I U S *(Shouting)*: And why the hell did he get so stingy?!
If a man just once a year! . . . Specially if you're in for life! . . .
Started feeling mean, did he? Stingy and mean. *(Calming
down)* That's a good one: begrudging a man giving his rod a
shake once a year. That's a good one.

T U L L I U S : Better than fathering orphans anyway.

P U B L I U S : Then don't send legions to Libya! Nor to Syria. Nor
to Persia.

T U L L I U S : A different matter altogether. *Dulce et decorum
est* . . . Noble and sweet. *Pro patria mori.*

P U B L I U S : Giving your rod a shake is sweet no less! And it's
also *pro patria*, more or less.

T U L L I U S : That's why they've stopped the visits. To prevent
confusion. To stop you getting them mixed up.

PUBLIUS: The sweet with the noble?

TULLIUS: The pleasant and the useful, Publius . . . A visit contradicts the whole idea of justice, the whole principle of the Tower. Especially the rod-shake. Tantamount to escaping from the Tower.

PUBLIUS: Escaping? While doing life? . . .

TULLIUS: It has nothing to do with you, Publius. Don't you see? Not with you, but with your sperm. *That's* an escape. More precisely, an emission. Learn to think abstractly, Publius. It's always the principle that counts. The idea that lies behind the thing, not the thing itself. Life term means life term. Life's the idea. Sperm's the thing.

PUBLIUS (*Shouting*): But I jerk off anyway. (*Calming down*) That cupboard's all yellow because of that . . .

TULLIUS: That's why they abolished them. To avoid mix-ups.

PUBLIUS: Mix up what?

TULLIUS: Things and ideas. As for the cupboard, we'll order you a new one. If, of course, you haven't grown attached to this one. Or vice versa.

PUBLIUS (*Measuring the cupboard with his eye*): No, I don't think so. Not terribly.

TULLIUS (*Picking up the receiver*): Hello, Mr. Praetor, sir. This is Tullius Varro in 1750. Yes, me again. Could you possibly send us a new bedside cupboard? Yes, preferably chromium steel. Yes, the old one—how should I put it?—rusted through . . . Yes, just one. Extremely obliged, Mr. Praetor, sir. Beg your pardon? What swan song? What? Whose last hurrah? I am ordering this for Mr. Publius Marcellus. What? Yes, he's embarrassed. Thank you. Much obliged. (*Puts the receiver down*) Soon it will be here.

PUBLIUS: Thank you.

TULLIUS: Nothing to it.

PUBLIUS (*Staring at the cupboard*): Should it be done right now, then?

T U L L I U S : Better right now. Out of sight, out of mind. D'you need help?

P U B L I U S *(Jealously)*: I'll do it myself!

T U L L I U S : As you wish . . . Only it's heavy . . . And what did you see in it? Especially since it's square-shaped . . .

P U B L I U S : Precisely that: that it's square-shaped. You just look around. Everything is rounded. Streamlined. Modernists! That's what they've done to Rome . . . Whereas in a square shape there is something that instills confidence. Something old-fashioned. The sum of angles. The idea of permanence. Of faithfulness. Something to get hooked by. Furniture! Mahogany. Something to carve initials in . . .

T U L L I U S : Sure. Or: "Publius plus Cupboard. Equals love." Although a tattoo would be even better. Depends, of course, where.

P U B L I U S *(Pensively)*: Yeah, a tattoo, of course, is more natural . . . *(Begins to heave the cupboard toward the chute)* Nothing's more natural than a tattoo. Especially if it's for life.

T U L L I U S : D'you need help?

P U B L I U S *(Grunting)*: It's okay . . . I'll do it myself . . .

T U L L I U S : "Myself, myself" . . . Don't give yourself a hernia.

P U B L I U S *(Groaning)*: Envious, aren't you? . . . Seeing a guy working . . . No, I'd better do it myself.

T U L L I U S : Jealousy, then . . . And I guess you're ticklish as well. Those who are jealous are always ticklish.

P U B L I U S *(Groaning over the cupboard table)*: You're repeating yourself, Tullius. Re-pea-ting. I've heard that one already. A year ago. On the other hand . . .

T U L L I U S : Yes, grab it from the other side. From the left . . .

P U B L I U S : On the other hand, it's hard to avoid repetition when it's for life. To a certain extent *(grunting)* to a certain extent, all that you can say . . . all that can be said *(groans)* . . . has been said already . . . By you or by me . . . I've heard it already . . . In some sense, this *is* a tattoo. *(Imitating* T U L-

LIUS's *voice*) "D'you need help," "I'll be sorry for you."

TULLIUS: Or *(imitating* PUBLIUS's *voice)* "I'll do it myself." I've heard that, too. And how many times! Like a recording. Like a tape or a camera. Or, worse still, on paper.

PUBLIUS: Well, that's what literature, frankly, is: a tattoo.
Black on white. And who knows what came first. That is, in
the beginning. Especially if it was the word.

TULLIUS: As I said: a barbarian. Stuffed with Holy Writ.

PUBLIUS *(Vehemently)*: And why then are they recording?!
(Pokes his finger to the ceiling and walls) Wasting tape. As
well as electricity.

TULLIUS *(Good-naturedly)*: Maybe they don't tape it. Maybe
they just do it live . . . D'you need help?

PUBLIUS *(Shudders, then reluctantly)*: Well, take it from the
left. I'll do it from the right and you from the left. If you are
not squeamish of course.

TULLIUS: Ah, never mind. I'll take it from the left. Just fine.
(In a tone of camaraderie) And it's nice that it's square-shaped.
Since it's so many-sided. Easier to carry.

PUBLIUS: That's why it's so sad *(groans)* to throw it away.
'Cause it's so many-sided.

TULLIUS: Sure. It unleashes the imagination. Variants and so
forth. The back side—look—is absolutely . . . well, pure. It
would be different if it were round.

PUBLIUS: The round is nice, too. Resembles a column. Body
in general. And those capitals, too . . . They're like hairdos.
Especially if you stare at them for a while. When I was young,
I could get a hard-on from looking at a column.

TULLIUS: And these days, it's square-shaped fare, right?

PUBLIUS: I wonder what came first: the square-shaped or the
round one? That is, what's more natural: the round one or the
square-shaped?

TULLIUS: Both, Publius, are artificial.

PUBLIUS *(Stops as if thunderstruck)*: Then—what was it in

the beginning? A triangle, huh? Or that—what's its name?—rhomboid?

T U L L I U S : In the beginning, Publius, you know, was the word. And the same will happen in the end. If you'll have time to utter it, of course.

P U B L I U S : In the end there will be something square-shaped. Quadrangular, to say the least.

T U L L I U S : If, of course, they don't cremate you . . . Urns, you know, come in great variety.

P U B L I U S : Depends on the Praetor, though . . . Lift it up a bit on the left.

T U L L I U S : Here?

P U B L I U S : Aha. Watch your hand.

(They lift the cupboard table and push it into the chute)

T U L L I U S *(Groans)*: E-e-ehhhh . . .

P U B L I U S *(Groans)*: E-e-e-hhhh . . .

T U L L I U S : E-e-ehhh—here she goes . . .

P U B L I U S : Sweetie . . .

T U L L I U S : Out of sight, out of mind.

(The cupboard table disappears)

P U B L I U S *(Staring down the shaft)*: I've heard that one already . . .

T U L L I U S : Don't get upset.

P U B L I U S : And this one, too . . .

T U L L I U S : Think that you've just pushed it overboard. And that we're on the ship.

P U B L I U S *(Clutching his ears with both hands, shouts)*: Shuuuuut up! *(Recovering himself)* I've heard that one as well. A year ago. Or the year before that. I don't remember. Well, it doesn't matter. It's not the words, it's the voice that

hurts! Yours, of course; but mine as well. And sometimes I just
can't tell yours from mine. It's like in wedlock, but worse . . .
All these years . . .

TULLIUS: Sure. And hence the erection . . . Well, I'll go wash
my hands . . . You'd better, too . . .

*(PUBLIUS covers his ears. Pause. TULLIUS disappears in the
bathroom, washes. Then he returns, walks toward the sofa, sits
down, and resumes his interrupted reading. PUBLIUS, with
his ears covered, stares for a while at the window; then he turns
around and returns to his alcove; sits down on the edge of his
bed and stares at the place where the cupboard table used to
be. Draws something with his finger on the floor, then wipes it
away with his foot. Raises the finger to his nose and stares at it:
dust. Gets up with a grunt and walks to the basin. Washes his
hands there and wipes them with the towel, very meticulously.
Takes a long time drying. Goes over to the birdcage. Opens it.
The canary doesn't fly out. Slams the door shut, then opens it
again. Nothing. Turns and goes over to the scales and weighs
himself very carefully. Removes his toga and weighs himself
again. Scrutinizes the result. Puts on toga, gets off the scales.
Sits down on his bed and records the results of the weighing)*

PUBLIUS: The toga, Tullius, you know . . . a good half kilo
in it.

TULLIUS: Mmmmmm. *(Continues reading)*

PUBLIUS: . . . 440 grams, to be exact. It's flannelette, that's
why . . . Although, come to think of it, what do we need togas
for in here? The temperature's constant. That's computers for
you . . . A normal one; ten degrees below body heat. No worries
about visitors, even guards. We ourselves, we don't go visiting
either . . . Overindulgence. An excess. Just stops you weighing
yourself properly. Tullius!

TULLIUS: What now?

P U B L I U S : What do we need these togas for? They're of no use at all. They just get in between your legs.

T U L L I U S : You're more like a statue that way. In Rome, everyone wears a toga. Read the rules. Letter *C*—Clothing. Toga and sandals.

P U B L I U S : But that's in Rome. Down there, you know, the weather changes. Strangers are everywhere, passersby. Broads. Whereas we're all family here. You and me, that is.

T U L L I U S : I told you: this way you're more like a statue. Especially if they chop your *kopf* off. Or the arms. So that you don't waste the furniture.

P U B L I U S : But I am like one anyhow *(undoes the toga)*, aren't I?

T U L L I U S : Stop that, will you, you are not in the Lupercalia . . . In a toga, what matters most? Folds. The world in itself, so to speak . . . living its own life. No relation to reality. Including the toga wearer. Not the toga for man, but man for the toga.

P U B L I U S : I don't get this at all . . . idealism or something . . .

T U L L I U S : Not idealism but absolutism. Absolutism of thought, get it? This is Rome's essence. To take everything to its logical end—and further. The rest—barbarism.

P U B L I U S *(Shouting)*: But how do you do it? What with? Where to? And what's it got to do with togas? Folds! . . . Their variety! A world in itself! They are just clothes. Starts with the letter C. Not the toga for man, say you, but man for the toga? Well, here I am throwing it away! *(Tears off the toga)* Well, what's it now? A heap of rags.

T U L L I U S *(Pensively)*: Looks like a stopped sea.

P U B L I U S *(Taken aback)*: You give me . . . too much reading . . . You give me the creeps.

(A lamp goes on over the rubbish chute. T U L L I U S *gets up and goes over to it. As he goes, he speaks to* P U B L I U S *over his shoulder)*

2 6

TULLIUS: Get dressed, don't frighten the cameras. *(Opens the hatch of the chute, a bust sails in)* Horace! Quintus Horatius Flaccus *in propria persona*! *(Tries to lift it)* Not the original but heavy. About fifty kilos in it, I guess. Publius! Come on, give us a hand.

(PUBLIUS puts on his toga and reluctantly helps TULLIUS to hoist the bust onto the shelf to join a dozen others)

PUBLIUS: Some poet—you could rupture yourself.

TULLIUS: All those classics are heavy. *(Wheezes)* Eh-h-h-h . . . Marble, that's why.

PUBLIUS: Marble because they're classics or—uuffffs—classics because they're marble?

TULLIUS: What are you implying? What does that mean, classics because they're marble? What are you driving at?

PUBLIUS: Just that marble's so solid. And it's not every blasted muzzle they bother to carve out of it. It's too resistant, I hear. Stab it or burn it, it's all the same. Maximum—the nose drops off. In time. Eventually. But that may happen even while one's still alive. Other than that, very tough material. And that's why they use it for statues: nothing doing.

TULLIUS *(Suddenly very interested)*: What-what-what, say it again . . .

PUBLIUS: Yeah, statues. Or maybe build yourself a bath. Like Caracalla. Although he could afford it, as an emperor. Since they always aim for posterity anyway. Emperors, that is. It's all show-off, of course, but then who's more abreast with which stone's more durable, right? Afterward, everything went metallic, iron, this and that . . . Selfishness, of course. Egotism. Nobody cares for posterity anymore. Take this very Tower, for instance. If it comes to that, it should have been made out of marble. Because this steel—how long is it going to last, for all

its chromium? A hundred years, say; well, two hundred . . .
What was Tiberius using for brains? . . . Ah, what's the use!
Besides, Horace himself . . . he talks about this very stuff . . .
what was it? . . . about getting himself a piece . . .

> I've raised a monument to
> myself, outlasting bronze . . .

The school stuff . . . sticks in your mind . . . as though it were
yesterday . . . Thick though he was, still he knew it's no use
playing with scrap iron . . .

T U L L I U S : Well, and?

P U B L I U S : And so it's only fair that they made this thing out
of marble. Even though it's just a copy. On the other hand,
with a copy it's not so sad if the nose drops off.

T U L L I U S *(Pensively, with a detached expression on his face)*:
Yes, not so bad if it's a copy.

P U B L I U S *(Lies down)*: Ooooof . . . some classic . . . Thank
heaven it's only a bust and not the whole statue. A toga alone
would weigh a . . . hate to think of it. Those folds of yours . . .

T U L L I U S *(Pensively)*: No, they don't carry statues. Busts only.

P U B L I U S : Pity. On the other hand, no broads make classics.
Only Sappho, and even she was AC-DC. And on top of that, a
toga . . .

T U L L I U S : Tunic.

P U B L I U S : What's that?

T U L L I U S : Like a toga, only shorter. Women, for instance,
wore it above the knee. Just covered the vital parts. Barely.

P U B L I U S : Good grief. Good grief, good grief, good grief . . .
Was that the fashion?

T U L L I U S : Not really. It's just that in Greece it's warmer.

P U B L I U S : Good grief. Above the knee.

T U L L I U S : Cool off, Publius.

P U B L I U S : Yeahhh . . . Greece . . . warm weather . . . Cypresses sticking up into the sky. Magnolias smelling. Laurel rustling. This Sappho, tunic above the knee. "My beautiful Pleiades have risen,/And I am alone in bed, I am alone . . ." End of the world.

TULLIUS: Yes, a good poet. Not a classic, though. Just fragments. Besides, a Greek.

PUBLIUS: A bust would do, though . . .

TULLIUS: Unlikely . . . they might suspect you of republican sympathies. All you need. May as well order Pericles. Or Demosthenes . . .

PUBLIUS: And just what can they do to us? . . . What else is there? . . . Well, increased surveillance perhaps . . . But we won't even be aware of that . . . The cameras, I guess, are everywhere anyway. The Tower's a TV mast as well . . . And a restaurant, on top of that . . . Hard to spot them, though . . .

TULLIUS (*Thoughtfully, glancing at the window*): It's crossed my mind several times, you know, that the window is but a camera. Disguised as a screen. Even when it's open. Especially then.

PUBLIUS: Aha, and all that cirrus-cumulus is just interference. Or rain . . . The sun as well.

TULLIUS: Yes, and the view of Rome is just a logo. To sharpen the focus; i.e., to distract the eye.

PUBLIUS: That's why the canary stays in.

TULLIUS: It isn't stupid . . . On the other hand, surveillance is natural. Even logical.

PUBLIUS: Oh, come off it. What's so logical about it? What are we capable of? What crime? Neither political, nor even street. Of course, I can slit your throat, I suppose. Or vice versa. But who is there to talk to, then? Of course, a replacement comes. Still, a replacement is a replacement . . . More of the same. The meaning of a crime lies in what? In consequences, in profits, in publicity, in them trying to catch you. In sentencing you when you're caught, and in imprisonment when you're sentenced. And us, we're locked up already. The reverse process is impossible. From the consequence to the cause. It won't work that way. That can't happen. So what's the use of cameras? Eh?

TULLIUS: Rubbish, Publius. A crime's only interesting outside of a context. When there is neither motive nor punishment. Half of world literature is about that.

PUBLIUS: But a crime outside of a context isn't a crime. Because only motive or punishment make it a crime!

TULLIUS: It? What it?

PUBLIUS: Well, it . . . the . . . act; action. Because everything in the world is defined by what's before and what's after. Without a before and an after, an event isn't an event.

TULLIUS: But what?

PUBLIUS: How should I know? Expectation. The state of "before." Of the procrastinating "after."

TULLIUS: Barbarian! Hopeless, unbearable barbarian. And he orders himself a Horace.

PUBLIUS: Stop barking at me, will you!

TULLIUS: Me barking? Barbarian, dumb senseless barbarian. Because an event without before and after is time. Pure and undiluted. A segment of it. A part—but of time. Something that lacks cause and consequence. Hence the Tower. And hence we in the Tower. Hence also the cameras: for what takes places in the Tower takes place in pure time. In its unadulterated, so to speak, version. As in a vacuum. That's why it's interesting. Especially if you knife me. Or if you don't. Even more interesting, then . . . Let them watch! Perhaps they'll understand something, a thing or two. Pity Tiberius didn't last longer: he'd have understood. This lot—Caligula, the Senate, and so on—how could they? Still, Rome won't end with them. That's why they record it on tape . . . All the same *(in a piercing whisper, as if in a trance),* all the same . . . even our descendants . . . hardly. What's happening to us can be understood only by us. And by no one else. For we—we possess time. Or it possesses us. It doesn't matter which. What matters is—no intermediaries. Between it and us—no one. Like when you lie on your back in a field in the evening and look up at a star. Nobody's between. Can't recall the last time that was. As a boy, I guess. But it feels like right now. "My beautiful Pleiades have risen, / And I am alone in bed," et cetera . . . What did this Sappho of yours know, anyway? Well, Greek is the word. Just a little egotist. Regarded infinity as loneliness. Egotist and cow. A Roman regards infinity as infinity. Against that, you can't shield yourself with no woman. Nor with anything, for that matter. And the more infinite it gets, the more Roman you are. It's for this that Tiberius erected this Tower . . . And you, thick-headed barbarian, are wasting such a chance. But it'll get even with you, one way or another. No way to avoid it for you, anyhow. Nor for the others either. Because Rome's destiny is to rule the world. As the poet has it.

P U B L I U S : Which one?

T U L L I U S : Virgil. And Ovid as well.

P U B L I U S *(Scanning the bookshelves and niches)*: Those, I guess, we've got already.

CURTAIN

ACT II

Same cell; after dinner. It's getting dark outside. P U B L I U S *is picking his teeth with a toothpick. On his head, earphones; apparently he's listening to music (fingers conducting occasionally).* T U L L I U S *is in an armchair rustling a newspaper. A picture of peace and well-being.*

P U B L I U S *(Squints suspiciously, turns his head left, then right; then pulls off earphones)*: I thought I heard the canary. Or did I imagine it?

T U L L I U S: You're hearing things.

P U B L I U S: I'm sure I heard the canary singing. Odd . . . Are you telling me the truth?

T U L L I U S: Oh, go to . . .

P U B L I U S: Perhaps they've released some Forest Aroma into the cell. *(Sniffs the air)* Although that's only on Fridays . . . Tullius!

T U L L I U S: Well, what is it?

P U B L I U S: What day of the week is it?

T U L L I U S: No idea. Something like . . . Wednesday.

P U B L I U S: Since they abolished years under Trajan, the weekdays, too, became somehow . . . you know . . . like fingers . . . nameless. I mean, it's better of course that we gave up those ordinal numerals. Because after the year 2000 there is somehow no point in counting them any longer. Even after the one thousandth everything is pretty senseless. Up to one thousand you're still counting, then you fall asleep . . . And who's there to count it for, anyway? 'Cause it's not money, no way to leave it—or touch it, either . . . And the whole trend—counting, that is—got started, I guess, for lack of better things to do . . . Although we, for instance, don't count . . . although there isn't much to do either . . . Most likely, they had some space to measure . . . Unlike here . . . That is, distance . . . So-and-so many days of journey . . . And so it went, by inertia. Just couldn't stop. One thousand. Two thousand. And so on . . . Even when kilometers were invented . . . Thanks to Trajan, got back to sense! For wherever you'd go, it was still the Empire. Now let the computers do it. Otherwise what is it—a thousand years, a thousand kilometers . . . Crazy . . . Pity about the names, though . . . Wednesday, Friday . . . That one—how d'you call it?—Thursday . . . Tullius? Sea Breezes—we get that on Thursdays, right?

T U L L I U S : On Tuesdays.

P U B L I U S : Lovely name, Tuesday . . . Still, how come I heard that canary? . . . *(Goes over to the cage, opens the door, talks to the canary)* Well now, did you or did you not? Sing, I mean. Eh? What's the story? Why the fuck are you silent? Can't understand human language, is that it? Liar, you understand everything. If I can hear you, you can hear me as well. Simply who cares, right? Just a meat mountain quivering, right? You, feathery-weathery . . . Or maybe you haven't been fed, eh? Tullius there has left a whole half truffle for you. Pure chocolate. From Gaul. And you, bitch, turn your beak off. Not kosher enough, eh? Gone on hunger strike, right? Well, Rome won't collapse over that. Even if Tullius and I did, it won't. And how can one do it anyway when it's all the time either cockscombs with horseradish or flamingo eggs stuffed with caviar? . . . Makes one doubtful, willy-nilly. Ulti-titi-ti-ti-tiuuuu. Well, never mind, you'll sing, you can't help it . . . Just follow our example, Tullius and me . . . Tullius!

T U L L I U S : What is it?

P U B L I U S : Maybe she's stopped singing because it's high up, after all? Almost a mile above sea level. They don't fly at this height. Let alone, chirp.

T U L L I U S : Well, ask her. Since you're talking to her anyway, aren't you? St. Francis . . . in disguise.

P U B L I U S : Doesn't answer. Clammed up and won't squeal. Like a crook or a left-winger. *(To the canary)* Uli-ti-ti-ti-

tiuuuuu? Are you a crook or a left-winger? Well, doesn't matter. Besides, neither is kept in the Tower anymore, right? Nowadays crooks and left-wingers prowl piazzas or sit on the Capitoline. 'Cause everybody's a bit of a crook and a bit left-wing. Some more, some less. It's a question of degree, not of substance. And to lock one up for the degree, let alone for substance . . . where d'you get towers enough, right? So you're here for no reason as well, sweetie . . . just here. Because of the Tiberian reform. So, more reason to follow our example, sister. See, we're prattling, aren't we? Even though you can't understand. But that's precisely why you should follow us. That's not a big deal, to follow somebody when everything's crystal clear.

TULLIUS: Oh, leave the bird alone! You're obsessed with it.

PUBLIUS: Just why is it that she won't imitate us, Tullius? Since she's in here as well! Otherwise it looks as if nature's against us! Since she represents nature, doesn't she? All the rest round here is artificial! Including us! Only she's natural, she alone . . .

TULLIUS: Don't get worked up . . . Represents, represents . . . Even if she does, it's just a lower stage of evolutionary development.

PUBLIUS: That's exactly what I mean. Even a parrot could be better. When my cohorts were stationed in Libya, in Leptis Magna, I knew one hetaera there. You know what that snake thought up? Kept an aquarium next to the bed. So that the fish, says she, got an education. To speed up evolution, that is. Otherwise, she says, too much of their roe gets wasted. Scattered, I mean. Well, and so I wonder why doesn't the damned bird ape us? Clammed up and won't budge . . .

TULLIUS: Perhaps if we'd get her a mate . . . Call the Praetor.

PUBLIUS: Well, *that* she won't learn from us. Maybe the other way around.

TULLIUS: Still itching, is it . . . Well, brace yourself for a little more: the walk's coming in five minutes. (*Stretches his arms*)

To shake your juice somewhat. So that it won't get churned into cheese.

P U B L I U S : Crude man you are, Tullius. Crude, but observant. *(Nods at newspaper)* What's in it, anyway?

T U L L I U S : A-h-h-h . . . usual rubbish. Skirmishes in Persia, hurricane in Oceania . . . Also a bit on the landing on Sirius and Canopus.

P U B L I U S : And?

T U L L I U S : No traces of life.

P U B L I U S : I could have told that without the trouble. Obvious even to the naked eye.

T U L L I U S : That is.

P U B L I U S : If there *was* life there, we wouldn't bloody well see them. At night especially. At night they go to bed and put the lights out . . . Life: what do they know about it . . . Experts.

T U L L I U S : And you, Publius? What can you tell about it? What is it—life, that is—according to you, eh?

P U B L I U S : It's when you slam the light out and grab a chick and . . . That's what life is . . . Oh, couldn't they hurry up with that walk!

T U L L I U S : Well, in this drivel of yours, no matter how wild it sounds, there is a grain of truth . . . But then, as the poet has it, *vox populi vox Dei* . . . The voice of the people is the voice of God . . . Or: The sober mind speaks the tongue of the drunk . . . Because, frankly, darkness indeed is a form of life. The condition of light, so to speak, only passive. By day, active; at night, passive. But, nevertheless, light. And what's light for our humble selves? A form of energy, a source of life. For a tomato, at least, or for a spring onion. And darkness is a source as well. Of the same thing. Of life. Of, as they call it, matter . . . And if it were only matter to reckon with, that would be fine. But for them, matter isn't enough, fabric isn't enough . . . No, they demand buttons, too, and so that they shine . . . Since life, in their view, is *quelque chose solide*, palpable, made out of meat. Fibers plus tissues. Molecules *cum* atoms. Stretch the hand and touch the stuff. *Quelque chose palpable* and subject to description. Or—to be photographed. Always out there . . . Whereas life is the texture things exist in. Not they themselves but their—what d'you call that? no, not tedium—medium. Medium, tedium, *Te Deum, per diem.* Tuesday and Thursday. Friday as well . . . It's not those stars of theirs but what's in between.

P U B L I U S : No need to get upset. It's just a newspaper. And anyway, it's only slobs who care for stars . . .

T U L L I U S *(Continuing)*: Not life for things: things for life . . . *(Calmer)* I wonder how they determine its absence. What with? A mine detector, or what? A Geiger counter?

P U B L I U S : Maybe they've outfitted a mine detector with the idea of Christianity. And of paganism. And of Buddhism and Islam . . . Could be anything . . . Who knows what they are up to. Hard to keep track . . . The new cupboard, mind you, they haven't sent it yet. Should I give the Praetor a ring?

T U L L I U S : Might arrive around bedtime. Should suit you fine. With the lights out, I mean.

P U B L I U S : You are a rude man, Tullius.

(First bars of "Tales of the Vienna Woods"; overhead lighting dims and the floor starts to move. Projected either from the wings or through the window, on all three walls of the cell, appears the image of a park with paths, a pond, statues. This picture may be static, better if it's a film; better still if the change of frames is coordinated with the movements of P U B L I U S *and* T U L L I U S)

P U B L I U S : Well, at long last. What have we today? The Villa d'Este or the Villa Borghese?

T U L L I U S : No-o . . . Looks like somewhere in Gaul. The Tui-
leries, isn't it? No more likely, that's in northern Scythia . . .
How d'you call it—in Eastern Europe . . . That is, in Western
Asia. What do they call that shtetl of theirs? . . .

P U B L I U S : Oh, God knows. A nice garden, anyway. There, you
see, Vertumnus and Pomona.

T U L L I U S : Aha, and this is *The Rape of the Sabines.*

P U B L I U S : That's it. And there's *Saturn Devouring His Child.*
Ye-e-es, some subject, as diets go . . . And the fence is nice, too;
terrific grillework. Even got swans over there . . . I wonder
where they got swans from.

T U L L I U S : *A* swan.

P U B L I U S : And what's this? *(Goes to the wall and pokes it with
his finger)*

T U L L I U S : Reflection. There is no swan without a reflection.
Like man without a biography. As the poet says:

> A swan sails through the ages' repetitive din,
> Admiring its faithful competitive twin.

P U B L I U S : Who said that?

T U L L I U S : I forget. Some Scythian. Observant tribe, that. Especially when it comes to animals.

(Pause; they stroll about)

P U B L I U S : That's what's interesting about poets: after them
you don't feel like talking. That is, don't feel as if you can.

T U L L I U S : Like talking crap, you mean?

P U B L I U S : No, talking *per se.*

T U L L I U S : One gets ashamed of oneself. Is that what you
mean?

P U B L I U S : Sort of . . . Of the voice, of the body, and so on . . .
Like after those lines about the double . . . Go on, say them
again.

A swan sails through the ages' repetitive din,
Admiring its faithful competitive twin.

P U B L I U S : The end of the road . . .

(Pause; they stroll about)

P U B L I U S : No reason to live, to go on. Perhaps to live was un-
necessary in the first place . . . although it's a habit . . . and
that's why they make children. Or out of ignorance! Not
knowing that *this* already exists . . . Or through poor contra-
ceptives . . .

T U L L I U S : Or hoping that they'll write verses, too. And some
try. But they soon switch to prose. Spouting in the Senate.
And so forth.

P U B L I U S : I too . . . indulged myself . . . When our cohort was
stationed in Libya . . .

T U L L I U S : Again some smut.

P U B L I U S : No, no, I was still young then . . . I wrote one, too . . .
Don't remember the whole thing, just two lines . . . about a
bird as well:

But when I had a fit of blues
A peacock feather was no use.

T U L L I U S : Not bad. Not bad at all, Publius. Not devoid of
elegance . . . Didn't you keep it up?

P U B L I U S : For a while. *(Declaims)*

Our grub is bland, the drink is stale.
I came to dread a peacock's tail.

T U L L I U S : Well, it has some atmosphere, hasn't it?

P U B L I U S : Do you really think so? That's exactly what I was
after: the atmosphere. *(Declaims)*

More withered, yes. Alas, no wiser.
A peacock's tail won't thrill me either.

Strange how they come to mind, these things . . .

T U L L I U S : And then what?

P U B L I U S *(Ruefully)*: Then I quit.

T U L L I U S : Pity . . . And not just because you might have been sitting now not here but in your own villa on Janiculum. Though *your* bust would get here eventually anyway . . . It's a pity, because what's said by a poet isn't repeatable, whereas what's said by you is. That is, if you are not a poet, your life's a cliché. Since everything's a cliché: birth, love, old age, death, the Senate, war in Persia, Sirius and Canopus, even Caesar. While the swan and its twin aren't. What's good about Rome is that there've been so many poets. Caesars, of course, too. But history is not them, it's what's said by the poets.

P U B L I U S : Oh yeah? And what about Tiberius and Trajan? The new territories in Africa?

T U L L I U S : To slit a throat, Publius, well, even a legionary can master that. And to die *pro patria*, too. As well as to expand the territory. As well as to suffer . . . But all that's cliché. That, Publius, has taken place already. Worse still: that will take place again. Anew, that is. In that sense, history doesn't have that many options. As well as its subjects. Because man, you know, is limited. One can squeeze out of him only so much. Like milk from a cow. Only five liters, for instance, if it comes to blood. He, Publius, is predictable. Like the house that Jack built, like a vicious circle. *Da capo al fine.* Whereas the poet starts where his predecessor has finished. It's like a ladder except that you start on the last rung, not the first. And the next one, well, you have to hammer it up yourself . . . For instance, in that Scythia of theirs, whoever grabs the quill now has to start precisely with that swan. Has to pull his quill, in a manner of speaking, from that white body . . .

P U B L I U S *(Looking closely at the landscape on the wall)*: I wonder if it is a film, or is it live?

TULLIUS *(Exploding)*: Who gives a damn! Nature is just nature! All those trees with their leafage! There you are, speaking of cliché . . . Trunks can still be told apart, but leaves . . . This, I suppose, is where the concept of majority came from . . . Nature herself is a live broadcast . . . From the Senate Hall . . . Endless ovation . . .

PUBLIUS: Don't get so upset about it, Tullius, so edgy. You know, lately you've really been on a short fuse . . . If you like, we'll switch it off. That's in our power.

TULLIUS: Yes, turn it off . . . ghastly rubbish, anyway . . . tautology . . . Ghastly treadmill. Tuned to your shuffling . . . Some exercise! Some back and forth! And on top of that, it's not clear what's tuned to what: your shuffling to the view—or the view to your shuffling!

PUBLIUS: Are you trying to define reality? It's just a treadmill. So that we have some exercise . . .

TULLIUS: And how do you know that reality is not a treadmill?! That it's out there just for your exercise's sake? And how do you tell reality from an exercise, anyway?

PUBLIUS: Well, by turning it off, I guess.

TULLIUS *(Screams)*: So do it! Whatever that is! Reality or exercise! Or both. For this is a tautology. Everything that has to do with space is a tautology! The worst part, it's natural! Mother, so to speak, Nature! . . .

PUBLIUS: Turniiiiiiing! *(Presses the button; the floor stops, the garden paths disappear, lights go on)* Next time better refuse in advance. *(Peaceably)* Next time . . .

TULLIUS: Barbarian! Next time! How d'you know what it's going to be, the next time? . . . You've come to take the arrival of tomorrow too much for granted. You've gone to seed!

PUBLIUS: What are you hinting at? That you're going to slit my throat? Here, slit! Do my bel canto a favor! Especially as it'll be on tape. Or even live. Go on, slit! Anything would be better than rotting in this stinking cylinder!

T U L L I U S : Nobody's interested in your throat . . . wash the floor afterward . . . keep that in mind . . . Lost my temper, I guess. You, too. Could be they've mixed some junk in that pâté.

P U B L I U S : You're fudging . . . although the pâté was indeed crummy . . .

T U L L I U S : On the other hand, we haven't tried that stuff before. Ostrich liver with raisins. Bloody cliché barkers . . .

P U B L I U S : On the whole, there hasn't been much fish lately.

T U L L I U S : Perhaps it's all gone to your madame, in Leptis Magna. To study evolution.

P U B L I U S : Or the naval blockade. You said yourself there's fighting in Persia.

T U L L I U S : It's summer as well. Goes bad quickly.

P U B L I U S : Mm—yeah. I wouldn't say no to a nice bit of fish now. Nice and fresh . . . *(Looks out the window)* Can't stand them stars, really. It would be much better to do time in the mines, under the republic . . . Nothing but coal all around . . . or uranium . . . But at least while cutting it, you had an illusion you were paving your way to the light . . . That's a nice idea, of course, extracting energy from the air. All these new neat ideas. Those mechanical lungs and livers that Tiberius introduced. And it's nice that that so-called blood is brown-colored. Not only economic but aesthetic independence as well, from the nomads with all their oil. Besides, more appropriate to Rome with its terracotta . . . Yet the mine, I reckon, was still better. None of these hopes, I mean, unwittingly linked to transparency . . . All this blueness . . . distance . . . hills. Umbria, the Alps. Specially in fine weather. What's more, in spring . . . Ultramarine and all that. For the hazel-eyed, this sort of thing is really deadly . . . When your gaze runs on and on . . . nonstop . . . Daydreaming develops . . . Unlike in the mines. This, I guess, was what Tiberius counted on. That instead of climbing walls, imagination would get unleashed . . . At the expense of anger, naturally . . . And on top of that, these stars . . . Vega and Cassiopeia, Orion and Ursa Major. One just can't concentrate. Plus Sirius . . . A bit more of that, and you find yourself rhyming twins and swans . . . It's a wonder you haven't taken it up, Tullius. With such a view . . .

TULLIUS: I have. As recently as yesterday.

PUBLIUS: Well?

TULLIUS: The view is fine, the view is fun
The view is 9.81.

PUBLIUS: Nine point eighty-one? What's that?

TULLIUS: Acceleration in free fall.

PUBLIUS: Macabre. And if you multiply it by a mile and a quarter . . . Macabre . . . So you think of it, too?

TULLIUS: Of what?

PUBLIUS: Well, about that . . . *(Indicates the ceiling with his eyes)* You know . . .

TULLIUS *(Looks at the ceiling)*: Up there—there is only that . . . what is it? . . . the restaurant. And the TV aerial.

PUBLIUS: No, no, I meant . . . *(Interrupts himself. A desperate pantomime follows. Rolling his eyes upward,* PUBLIUS *simultaneously jabs his index finger downward. Then, having realized that the meaning of his gesticulation doesn't reach* TULLIUS, *changes his tactics and, jabbing the finger toward the ceiling, squints his eyes toward the floor. After this follows a combination of both, as a result of which he gets totally confused and, realizing this, shouts—a mixture of whisper and shriek)* About escape! . . . Or . . . Or . . . *(his eyes widen)* or suicide!

TULLIUS: A very noble Roman tradition, that . . . Seneca and Lucretia. Mark Antony . . . All the same, why should I consider suicide, eh?

PUBLIUS: Why, what do you mean? . . . It's . . . It's . . . It's a way out! An exit!

T U L L I U S : Suicide, Publius, is not a way out. It's no exit, it's just the word "Exit" painted on a wall. As the poet said: As simple as that.

P U B L I U S : What poet?

T U L L I U S : I don't remember. An Easterner.

P U B L I U S : Where's that?

T U L L I U S : In Western Asia, too. An observant people they are . . .

P U B L I U S : In that case . . . *(Runs to the washbasin, turns the tap on, and speaks in a piercing whisper)* It's about—escape?

T U L L I U S : You're an absolute savage, dear Publius. Escape, suicide. Are you in kindergarten? Escape to where? To Rome— from the Tower? That's like escaping from history into anthropology. Better still, from time into history . . . Degradation, to put it mildly. From time, more exactly, into space. One'd be bored to death.

P U B L I U S : Is here any better? There, at least, something's going on in space, I mean. Cock fighting. Hetaeras. Gladiators. The Senate, after all. The legislative process. Or I'd join the Legion again. To hell and all! To Libya, Persia! For one who's not a poet, there is still history. To play a part in. Or at least in geography. Especially when you go by sea.

T U L L I U S : That can be seen from here as well. In fine weather especially.

P U B L I U S : Sure. The cockfights, too . . . On the video, tape-recorded. For posterity.

T U L L I U S : Or live. Shall we switch on?

P U B L I U S : Ah, forget it.

(Lamp goes on above elevator)

T U L L I U S : Publius!

P U B L I U S : What?

TULLIUS: Your wife has arrived.

PUBLIUS: Eh?

TULLIUS: Your new cupboard. I think it's here.

PUBLIUS *(Noticing lamp and rising from the sofa)*: You are a crude man, that's for sure.

TULLIUS: Need any help?

PUBLIUS: I'll manage. *(Opens hatch: a new, chromium steel cupboard sails in)*

TULLIUS: A beauty, eh?

PUBLIUS: Not bad at that.

TULLIUS: The same texture as the Tower itself. Not just any old thing.

PUBLIUS: Mm—yes . . . Not bad. Except that everything is reflected in it. *(Places the cupboard next to his bed, takes two steps back)* Like a distorting mirror. But still a mirror.

TULLIUS: There's no swan without a reflection . . . Well, this may cool you down a bit. Southern temperament. Or it may inflame you, for the same reason . . .

PUBLIUS: Oh, come on . . . Envious, aren't you? Of course, at your age . . . well, at mine, too . . . Time was you stuck your penis in a bucket, the water would boil . . . And now, well. *(Waves his hand wearily)*

TULLIUS: I could carry a bucket on mine, from the first floor to the fifth. At the crack of dawn especially, with the first rooster . . .

PUBLIUS: Stop bragging, will you.

TULLIUS: A bet?

PUBLIUS: What with?

TULLIUS: Your sleeping pills. A week's supply.

PUBLIUS: Find a bucket first. They don't make them anymore . . .

TULLIUS: Well, just a call to the Praetor; he'll dig one up . . .

PUBLIUS: And a staircase . . . *(Pause;* PUBLIUS *investigates the cupboard's interior)*

T U L L I U S: It's odd how things go out of fashion. That very bucket, for instance.

P U B L I U S: Well, I suppose they still use them in rural areas, in the countryside. In Libya, for example.

T U L L I U S: But that's in Libya . . . If it weren't for you, I wouldn't even think of Libya. Or of rural areas . . . of the world . . . Well, something rather horizontal. Greenish-brown *cum* blue. Dales and vales, townships and hamlets. All those little cubes and triangles. Crosses and naughts. Tiny blue threads. Fields, furrowed or plowed . . .

P U B L I U S: Let's call the Praetor, eh? And get a map of the Empire?

T U L L I U S: Or wallpaper. Which is the same thing . . . The meaning of the Empire, Publius, is in rendering space meaningless. When so much is conquered, it's all the same. Be it Persia, Sarmatia, Scythia, Libya, Gaul—what's the difference? Tiberius, actually, was the first to sense that . . . And those space programs, they are, too, more of the same, for what do they end with? With a cohort on Sirius, a colony on Canopus. And then what? Come back. Because it's not man who conquers space but space that exploits man. Since it's inescapable. You turn a corner thinking there's another street. But it's just the same street, for it is—in space. That's why they embellish porticos—all that plaster and things, put on numbers and fancy names. So as not to think about this horrid horizontal tautology. Because everything is an enclosure, a room. Floor, ceiling, four walls. North and south, east and west. With all these square feet. Or cubic ones, if you like that better . . . For every room is a cul-de-sac, Publius, a dead end. Big or small, painted with cockerels or rainbows, but a dead end. A john, Publius, differs from Persia only in size. Worse still, man himself is a dead end. For he, too, is an enclosure. Six feet high at best by one foot in diameter. Cubic or anatomic ones, whatever they measure those volumes with . . .

PUBLIUS: You mean, a space within a space, right?

TULLIUS: Aha. A thing in itself. A cage inside a cell, as the canary would put it. An oasis of horror in a desert of boredom. As the poet has it.

PUBLIUS: Which one?

TULLIUS: Gallic . . . And everyone's the same. Anatomically, that is. Doubles and twins. Swans. Nature, Publius, is a mother in the sense it has no truck with variety. Say, you get an idea of doing the town, but just a look at the mirror and—forget it. Or at that cupboard there . . . never mind, it's distorting . . . That's why they grab those florid rags, motley togas . . .

PUBLIUS: Tunics.

TULLIUS: Chitons.

PUBLIUS *(Keenly)*: What's that?

TULLIUS: Outer garb, lightweight. Like a tunic, but over it . . . Greek as well . . . doesn't matter. The main thing is not to bump into yourself, not to recognize the enclosure. The whole horror of it is that people have much more in common than otherwise. And the difference expresses itself only in centimeters. *Kopf*, arms, legs, the crucial organ; the tits if a woman. But from the spatial point of view, Publius, from the spatial point of view even mounting a dame is something unisexual. Not to speak of a gent. A sort of topographical perversion takes place, toposexualism if you like. Tautology. And Tiberius grasped it precisely because he was—Caesar. Because he's used to regarding his subjects en masse. Because Caesars—what d'you think they are always after? They're after a common denominator.

PUBLIUS: Well, I think it was the Emperor of China to whom it occurred first. His subjects have much more in common than others, don't they? Both denominator and numerator. That's why, I guess, they've never got themselves even a republic. One represents all.

TULLIUS: Oh, but there are a billion plus of them, Publius.

Even though one senator per million was elected, can you imagine what sort of a senate that would be? Eh? Or the results of voting? Say, 70 percent for and 30 percent against? That means a minority of three hundred million.

PUBLIUS: Yeah, some have become Caesars on a lot more modest grounds.

TULLIUS: That's not the point! That's not the point, Publius! Not the number! Sure, a billion by itself is space. Especially if you put them shoulder to shoulder. But on top of that, they mount each other. Copulate. A form of space which is not only expanding but has a knack for self-reproduction. That's why they carve each other up with such indifference in the Orient. Because there are a lot, and whatever you have a lot of is interchangeable. That one—what's his name?—who ran Scythia? the last century of Christianity? or rather post-Christianity? Well, anyway, he proclaimed exactly that: with us, he said, no one is irreplaceable . . . But the point is not numbers, the point is space that devours you. Disguised either as a mile or as someone else in your own likeness. And there is no escape from that, no place to hide, except into time. That's what Tiberius had in mind. He alone understood it. Neither the Chinese Emperor nor the Eastern satraps did. Only Tiberius. And hence the Tower. For it's nothing but a form of struggle against space. Not just against horizontality! No, against the idea itself! For it reduces enclosure to a minimum. It virtually pushes you out physically. Into time. Into pure time, not mucked up by miles and kilometers; into Chronos. For the absence of space is the presence of time. To you this is a cell, jail, dungeon—because you are a barbarian. Barbarians are always such suckers for *Lebensraum* . . . to keep the limbs limber . . . the dust from settling . . . For a Roman, though, this is a device for comprehending time. For penetration into it . . . and a device, mind you, nearly perfect, with all its life-support systems included.

PUBLIUS: Yeah, that's for sure. The end of the line. That's to say, this cell can't be beat.

TULLIUS: Solitary, though, might be better. There's even less space there. Especially anatomical . . . Beyond that, of course, there is only a coffin. Where space comes to an end, and you become time yourself. Cremation, though, would be even better, but that, of course, is up to the Praetor.

PUBLIUS: And where does the urn with the ashes go? To the relatives?

TULLIUS: I'd prefer the chute. At least that way it gets to the Tiber. What's more, no room is wasted. Space, that is . . . Up to the Praetor, though.

PUBLIUS: No, I'd say to the relatives . . . At least Octavian will know where his daddy is stashed away. Otherwise it's as if I never existed. Otherwise the only proof for him is my pension . . . Whereas it wasn't through the Holy Ghost only . . .

TULLIUS: Yes, Tiberius didn't like those long frocks, not at all . . .

(Pause)

PUBLIUS: If you'd let me, we could reduce space. Under the same blanket, eh?

TULLIUS: Sure, some reduction. By five inches.

PUBLIUS: Eight! Should I show you?

TULLIUS: Come off it. I've seen it. Six if you strain it.

PUBLIUS: Eight! Want to bet?

TULLIUS: For your sleeping pills.

PUBLIUS *(Retreating)*: The diameter, though! circumcised, too . . . Six inches you know . . . doesn't grow on trees either.

TULLIUS: Besides, it wouldn't be a reduction, it would be an increase.

PUBLIUS: Even if only by five inches?

TULLIUS: Even if only by five.

PUBLIUS: Ah well, keep it, then . . . Who wants it, anyway? *(With irritation)* The world doesn't end in your sphincter . . . Big deal . . . When our cohort was stationed in Libya, I knew an Arab. Well, for a couple of sesterces he'd let you—but in the nostrils. He, too, was pretty choosy, conserved space and all that. And when a client came, he'd snuffle it up . . . He died of catarrh of the upper bronchial system . . . there.

TULLIUS: You'd better ring home, Publius. Chat with a family.

PUBLIUS: Ring yourself! Home! . . . where you won't be back, ever. You may just as well call ancient Greece! Or Biblical Judea . . . "home." Why don't you say "mama," too? . . . I'd send them that urn right now . . . they wouldn't even bother checking. To them, "for life" means a great deal more than it does here. Because down there is where life goes on . . . While here . . . Let's play chess, eh? Black or white?

TULLIUS: The chessmen, Publius, were swapped for Horace a while ago.

PUBLIUS: Ah-h . . . I'd clean forgotten. My head is getting . . .

TULLIUS: You should go easy on that cupboard.

PUBLIUS: How about fencing a bit?

TULLIUS: So late? As the girl said to the legionary.

PUBLIUS: Yeah, true . . . Is it going to be like this all the time, eh? Always? Really till "the end of our days" . . . And when is that to come? Considering that diet of theirs . . . And when it comes, they say you don't notice . . . Always, then . . . In ten years. In twenty. When we won't have any strength left for fencing. Not to mention chess. And the entire cell will be full of busts . . . "Always," in other words, is when we'll forget how many there were today. Was Horace here or not . . . And I—I may forget about that even by tomorrow. Or the day after . . . Maybe tomorrow is precisely where "always" begins, eh? And maybe it's already started? *(Shouts)* Because I don't remember

how many of them there were yesterday! Sixteen? Fourteen?
With or without Horace? . . . One could go mad that way.

TULLIUS: That's precisely why they locked us up together. So
that wouldn't happen.

PUBLIUS: Eh?

TULLIUS: So that every thought would be divided by two.

PUBLIUS: Eh?

TULLIUS: Like in a marriage. Then again: they tape everything. And a thought divided by two is always more compre-
hensible . . . Not to mention less terrifying . . .

PUBLIUS: You mean . . . You mean we're here for . . . as . . .
as a lesson for posterity? . . . like guinea pigs?

TULLIUS: No, not at all . . . Besides, guinea pigs lack the power
of speech. They have to be interpreted . . . behaviorism, you
know . . . And no posterity will have time enough to bother
about us . . . To play those tapes . . . It's for life, you know . . .
It's just that some ideas don't fit in one head. They need—in
order to become a thought—more than one brain. Two heads
are better than one: folk wisdom: to think a thought through—
the theory of relativity, for example, or this "always" of yours.

PUBLIUS: But this means . . . this means that we are becoming
one brain. From the idea's point of view, that is. Wherever it
settles becomes its brain. A left and right hemisphere.

TULLIUS: I'd better be the left one.

PUBLIUS: So why can't we lie in one bed, then! One brain, one
body, one bed.

TULLIUS: The whole point is, one body could go out of its
mind but two won't. At least not because of the same thought.

PUBLIUS: Turning it down, then . . . So much for your solitary
this, solitary that . . . One idea for two, and under one blanket—that would be a real solitary confinement.

TULLIUS: Well, your "always" won't cover enough, I tell you.
Not for two, anyway, that's for sure.

PUBLIUS: Eh?

TULLIUS: Because you're an egotist, that's why. Like all barbarians. This "always" of yours concerns you and you only. It's not time, Publius, that you're talking about: you're just sorry for yourself. Self-pity, that's what it is. Yet with self-pity one can live. It's even pleasant. Whether I let you or not, you'd still be sorry for yourself. Even if a woman let you, even if a queer ...

PUBLIUS: Oh, you know everything, don't you?

TULLIUS: And so why did you do the rounds of all the brothels in that Libya of yours? Huh? You *did* have a woman, didn't you? As well as—what's his name?—your Octavian, huh? You weren't in the Tower, were you?

PUBLIUS: Are you saying I am here for being unscrew ... no, unscrupulous?

TULLIUS *(Continuing)*: You were always sorry for yourself, that's the thing. And you are now. And your "always" tells just how much you are. "Ah, it's going to be like that tomorrow and the day after! Oh, and yesterday was just the same! Oh, how miserable I am!" And so forth.

PUBLIUS: And you! What about yourself! *(Bursting out)* Do you remember how many busts there were here yesterday?

TULLIUS: No idea. Who cares? Fifteen. Sixteen ... And on the whole, I'd rather be the right hemisphere.

PUBLIUS: But I've remembered! I've remembered! Fourteen! There were fourteen of them!

TULLIUS *(Scanning shelves and niches)*: And there still are fourteen, including Horace.

PUBLIUS *(Agitated)*: Aha! Aha! That's because we ordered Seneca yesterday, and we didn't like him. And we sent him back, because of the beard. And today we got Horace—so there are fourteen again. There were fourteen, then it was thirteen, then it became fourteen again. *(Clasps his head)* Oh, what am I doing? ... I thought there were *fifteen*!

TULLIUS: Calm down, Publius, calm down. Addition and subtraction. What's the difference: It's just that they happen to be undertaken simultaneously. Whereas you're used to doing them in sequence. Big deal. How many busts! Like that water in the basin . . . Two pipes come in, one goes out . . .

PUBLIUS *(Desolate)*: I could never make any sense of that one . . .

TULLIUS: Neither could I . . . Speaking of which, let's order a swim—late as it is—instead of a shower.

PUBLIUS *(Continuing)*: That's . . . that's enough to drive you mad! 'Cause these busts . . . there's more and more of them! And there's going to be more!

TULLIUS *(Enigmatically)*: There may be more. Or none at all.

PUBLIUS *(Puzzled and suspicious)*: Just what do you mean by that?

TULLIUS *(Recollecting himself)*: The classics . . . er . . . er . . . there's not all that many of them, anyway. The Roman ones, I mean. One or two more, and you are through.

PUBLIUS *(Shouting out)*: Fifteen!

TULLIUS *(Continuing)*: The main thing: not to mix them up with the emperors. Ennius, Lucretius, Terence, Catullus, Tibullus, Propertius, Ovid, Virgil, Horace, Martial, Juvenal. Main thing, don't mix them up with emperors. Nor with the orators. Nor with playwrights. Only poets.

PUBLIUS: Because there's a shortage of marble.

TULLIUS: Nor with the Greeks. Nor, what's more, with the Christians. In your case, that's most important.

PUBLIUS: Why?

TULLIUS: Because for a barbarian it's always simpler to become a Christian than a Roman.

PUBLIUS: Eh?

TULLIUS: Out of self-pity, Publius, out of self-pity. Since you want to escape from here. Or—to commit suicide, right? That is, you crave life, preferably eternal. Eternal—but life it must be, right? You don't want to attach this adjective to anything else, do you? The more eternal, the more life, eh?

P U B L I U S : Well, what of it? What's wrong with that?

T U L L I U S : No, no, surely I didn't . . . no. There's nothing wrong with that. Quite the contrary. What's more, it's all manageable, Publius: escape, suicide; to gain eternal life as well. All that, Publius, is certainly possible. But this striving for the possible is precisely the *mauvais ton* for a Roman. And therefore, dear Publius . . .

P U B L I U S : What! How! What'd you say? . . . escape's possible? . . . eh? You said . . . did you say . . . it's manageable . . . Did I hear you right?

T U L L I U S : It's manageable, yes, it's manageable. Everything's manageable. Meantime . . .

P U B L I U S *(Jumping up and yelling)*: In what way? How? Where? *(Wildly looks around as though searching for a way out, as though suspecting that he has overlooked something; then rushes to the chute, to the elevator door, to the window—tests the glass with his palms—then throws himself to the bird-cage, as though struck by an idea, but at once turns away, disillusioned, etc. A two-minute-long pantomime, during which* T U L L I U S *, arms behind back à la schoolmaster, examines the busts)* How? Where? *(His excitement fades)* You're lying, you bastard! There's no chance. Not in this incarnation. And I'd crack your filthy mug . . . if I didn't have to face it for life . . . Scum. Bitch. Filthy bitch, that's what you are, Tullius. Old filthy Roman bitch. She-wolf. No scruples, no nothing. Making fun of a simple man. "Manageable, possible" . . .

T U L L I U S *(His pose unchanged)*: What do you want to bet?

P U B L I U S : Your sleeping pills.

T U L L I U S : Better yours. Mine are all finished.

P U B L I U S : Done . . . *(He begins to realize the idea behind the bet, but is too lazy to think it through)* Are you really . . . you've really . . . lost your marbles? . . . for if I lose . . . that is, if you win, then . . .

TULLIUS: In the meantime, Publius, repeat after me: Ennius, Terence, Lucretius . . . Well, come on!

PUBLIUS (*Repeats, bending his fingers to count*): Ennius, Terence, Lucretius . . .

TULLIUS: Catullus, Tibullus, Propertius . . .

PUBLIUS: Catullus, Tibullus, Propertius . . .

TULLIUS: Virgil, Ovid, Horace . . .

PUBLIUS: Virgil, Ovid, Horace . . .

TULLIUS: Lucan, Martial, Seneca . . .

PUBLIUS: Lucan, Martial, Seneca . . .

TULLIUS: Juvenal . . . ah, let's add some historians! Pliny, Tacitus, Sallust . . .

PUBLIUS: Pliny, Tacitus, Sallust . . . I feel sle-e-epy . . .

(Pause, during which the curtain descends a quarter)

TULLIUS: Take a sleeping pill. You've got some still . . . eh?

PUBLIUS: Indeed. Indeed, you're right . . . good idea . . . *(Leans his palm against his bed head's keyboard; "Publius Marcellus— No. 1750-A" flashes on the screen.* PUBLIUS *presses a button and "Request—sleeping pills" flashes up. Then from the opening next to the keyboard appears, as in a pneumatic pipe, an elongated cylinder, in which when* PUBLIUS *picks it up can be heard a characteristic rattle of tablets.* TULLIUS *follows all this manipulation as if mesmerized.* PUBLIUS *speaks with seeming satisfaction)* Say what you like, but my fingerprints aren't the same as your fingerprints . . . *(Shakes out several pills into his palm, walks over to the decanter standing on the table, throws the tablets into his mouth, and washes them down, drinking straight from the decanter)*

TULLIUS (*Swallowing spittle*): Roman computers . . . are famous for their hospitality. *(Lights a cigarette)*

PUBLIUS (*Disappears into lavatory; the sound of a powerful stream, then the roar of flushing, replaced with the sound of water running from a tap; he brushes his teeth, gargles water in his throat, mumbling at the same time names of classics):* Catullus, Tibullus, Propertius, Virgil, Ovid, and Horace. Catullus, Tibullus . . . *(He emerges from lavatory, crosses the stage on the way to his alcove, mumbling the names as he rearranges his toga around his crotch)* Propertius, Ovid, Virgil, Horace . . . *(Sits down in his alcove and begins to undo his sandals, and suddenly falls asleep in that position and rolls over on his side)*

(Long pause, after which T U L L I U S *gets up and goes over to* P U B L I U S*'s alcove; puts* P U B L I U S *to bed, all the time keeping his eye on the jar with the pills; takes it into his hand and reads the label; swallows spittle; puts the jar back; looks out of the window: the moon and stars are out.*

Pause: after which T U L L I U S *draws the curtain over* P U B- L I U S*'s alcove, walks over to a niche, and takes from there a bust of, say, Virgil and, creaking and grunting, stalks with it across the stage over to the chute and puts the bust down next to its opening, on what serves as a dining table; it's a sort of platform with a height regulator, as in hospitals; for the next few minutes* T U L L I U S *is busy carrying busts from shelves and niches and putting them down on the table; he perspires a great deal and gets short of breath. He strips down to the waist and, having stopped to catch his breath, listens for* P U B L I- U S*'s rather loud snoring)*

T U L L I U S *(Straightening up and wiping the sweat from his brow)*: Now, there is a man who knows how to squash a bedbug! That's what the arms of what's-his-name are all about. *(Quotes)* "Lesbia, where have you been? In Morpheus' arms I have rested . . ." Well, so Catullus is the first to go. In the first place, it's a copy, so there's not much to be sorry for . . . Sec-

ondly, he's far too popular . . . translated into all languages . . .
Heavy as an emperor as well . . . beats Horace at that . . . over
fifty kilos in it . . . And at the acceleration of 9.81 . . . and with
700 meters to go . . . that will settle the shredder . . . and indeed
the dear little crocodiles. That is, the dear little crocs will gorge
on marble . . . some diet . . . it's not mincemeat . . . that's different . . . that's no small way to get your dear little choppers
busted . . . And here, on top of that, we'll brush them a bit with
Virgil . . . especially because the likeness is so-so . . . and whoever saw him, anyway? . . . Maybe it's not even him . . . an
anonymous author. *(Declaims)*

> Smart skipping sheep will themselves graze on bluebells
>   in the meadow
> So we won't bother in winter dyeing their curly wool
>   blue . . .

Lovely, yes . . . well worth all that infinite *Aeneid (pushes
Virgil's bust to the chute)* . . . a heavy . . . it must be said . . .
poet . . . epic is the word . . . No, I for one . . . I wouldn't like
to be . . . the little crocodile . . . no sir . . . 35,000 kilogram-
mommeters at the moment of impact, no less . . . and at 500
kilometers per hour . . . And—smack on the snout . . . And if
that's somebody like, say . . . Lucretius . . . especially as he
couldn't care less . . . being crackers . . . *(Recites)* "Fortunate
is anyone who/comprehended the cause of existence" . . .
Oooofff . . . If only because the cause of existence compre-
hends . . . no, apprehends anyone who is fortunate . . . or
unfortunate . . . or how does it go? . . . *(Declaims)*

> There are a number of things whose existence prompts
>   many
> explanations and yet only one of them's true.
> Thus when you notice at times a breathless corpse in
>   the distance,

you'd be wiser to list all the possible causes of death.
For you're unable to prove whether he died of exposure,
of the sword, of malaise, was he poisoned perhaps.
What has happened to him was a thing of that nature
That's how we're likely to talk when we ponder the
     nature of things.

N-n-n-no . . . no desire to be a little croc on my part . . . And why not pep things up somewhat with *(heaves one more bust)* Tibullus . . . since he died young anyway . . . sang . . . mostly maidens . . . Delia and so forth . . . Or with Propertius . . . also mainly about Cynthia . . . who cares for you nowadays, brothers . . . Or better still, with Seneca . . . especially as he was a suicide . . . A terrific line that was . . . when he was still kicking his heels . . . about that island they'd sent him to . . . Corsica was it? . . . *(Declaims)*

    Here where the exile exists alongside his exile . . .

Very fitting. Considering these quarters . . . Ah, Publius, Publius, if you only knew the Roman poets . . . You'd be less nervous . . . And you'd hand me over your sleeping pills . . . without all this hassle . . . And I wouldn't have to sweat and slave here like a goddamn donkey. And the shredder would be left intact, and the dear little crocs, or the bundle of snakes, or whatever it is would be alive and well . . . But instead, what? Lucius Annaeus Seneca has to . . . as though suicide weren't enough . . . has to hobble downstairs at 500 kilometers per hour . . . That is, doing almost 130 meters per sec . . . And the same for Lucan . . . Marcus Annaeus Lucan . . . author of no more nor less than *Pharsalia* . . . partly, of course, as he's Seneca's nephew . . . and, of course, because he too committed suicide . . . young as he was . . . that is, opened his veins himself . . . saving Nero a trip . . . That line, incidentally . . . about those very veins of his . . . it wasn't bad . . . not bad at all . . . (*Recites*)

Ah, life never before ran such a widening road!

Brrrr, but well put. There've been good authors in Rome. On the heavy side, though . . . and one's to break one's neck heaving them around, because an ignoramus and barbarian is nonetheless counted as a Roman citizen and therefore is automatically covered by the Tiberian reform with all its consequences, the sleeping pills included . . . Leftovers from the republic, that's what it is . . . and what gets you is that the creep doesn't know a single line—neither Martial nor Juvenal nor Persius . . . just some schoolboy's Horace . . . yet all the same: takes sleeping pills . . . no spiritual life whatsoever, just plain metabolism and yet, no matter what, give him barbiturates of calcium! Democracy . . . And through all that such good lads (*gestures toward the busts*) lose their ears and noses . . . Ech! . . . a drink maybe . . . (*Heads toward the amphora*) One for the road, so to speak . . . "Fill my cup, beloved youngster, with the bitter Phalerian liquid" . . . (*Moves to the side, having filled his glass*) Well, you classics . . . The severed heads of civilization . . . The lords of the mind . . . How many times has literature been accused of helping people escape reality?! (*Drinks*) Well, it's high time to prove it. Time to descend from the clouds (*flings the chute door open*) to earth. From the stars, so to speak, back to the thorns. More accurately, to the Tiber's muddy waters . . . As the poet has it . . .

(*With these words* T U L L I U S *starts pushing the busts of the classics one after another down into the opening of the chute. Only two busts remain in the cell—Ovid and Horace.* T U L-L I U S *stuffs his mattress and pillows into the opening and, crab-fashion, climbs in himself*)

TULLIUS *(Addressing the remaining busts)*: I'd rather you didn't . . . You *(gently slapping Horace on the pate),* you haven't even settled in here yet . . . And you *(to Ovid)* . . . how does it go now? *Nec sine te nec tecum vivere possum* . . . Neither with you nor without you is life thinkable . . . True. Very true. *(With these words,* TULLIUS *holds his nose and disappears down the shaft)*

CURTAIN

ACT III

The same cell. Early morning. The rays of the sun pattern the ceiling, penetrating inside as though from below. Loud singing of the canary. This is what wakes P U B L I U S.

P U B L I U S *(Stretching in his alcove)*: U-li-tit-tit-tit-tyu-yu-yu-u, tyu, tyuu . . . Uli-tit-tit-tit-tyu-yuu-yuu, tyu, tyuuu . . . Tibullus, Catullus, Propertius . . . Tyuu, tyuu . . . you-u-u little bitch . . . you've resumed singing . . . You hear, Tullius . . . she has started . . . a? . . . Tullius? . . . Still asleep . . . Oh-h-h-h *(sits up in bed holding his head)*, oh-h-h . . . blasted barbiturates . . . they make themselves felt . . . Well, coffee, then . . . *(In an unconscious gesture, he presses his palm against the keyboard. The name, number of the cell, and the word "Request" flash up on the screen. Equally unconsciously,* P U B L I U S *presses a button—the word "Coffee" flashes up; his hand falls lifelessly as the characteristic sound of an espresso machine is heard and a smell of coffee drifts in the hall)* Uli-ti-tit-tyuuuu . . . Pretty good hard-on, eh? Well, how many centimeters are you, mister? . . . Ooooooh . . . Powerful stuff . . . Oooooh . . . Rrrrrrright now I could . . . Who said that, Nero or Claudius . . . some oldster . . . "Don't ever trust the prick erected in the morning: it craves no fuck, it wants a pee" . . . Oooooh . . . Ohboy-ohboy-ohboy-ohboy . . . *(Throws off the curtain and lowers his feet onto the floor. He sits thus for some time, then rises and heads for the lavatory: the same sounds that we heard at the end of the previous act. He comes out of the lavatory, returns to his alcove, sits down, pours coffee, gets up, goes over to the window, stretches, takes a first sip, gets a cigarette, and lights it up)* Lictors-and-praetors, what a day! The Tiber curving away, the hills looming blue. All Rome, damn it, is there under your nose! Pines rustling, every measly needle visible. Fountains sparkling like crystal chandeliers . . . The entire Empire lies in plain view, from Judea to Castricum . . . Makes you feel like a princeps . . . On the other hand, of course, it may be that they're just . . . putting it on . . . Eh, Tullius? What d'you think? . . . Still asleep, creepo . . . missing a day like this . . . Well, most likely it's live . . . but even if it's on tape . . . And they've taped it, I bet, 'cause it couldn't be better . . . no way! . . . *(Drinks coffee)* Tullius! . . . Hey, Tullius? Get up! How long are you going to loll around? . . . My, what a day! . . . Hey, Tullius! *(Turns around and only now notices something untoward: the absence of busts and the general disorder in* T U L L I U S *'s alcove)* Tullius? *(Rushes to* T U L L I U S *'s alcove)* Tullius, where are you? Tullius! Tullius!! *(With alarm turning to horror as he realizes that* T U L L I U S *has disappeared)* Tullius, where are you?! *(Rushes to the lavatory from which— he realizes on the way—he himself emerged a minute ago; looks under the bed, looks everywhere that a human body could be hidden)* . . . And the classics! . . . *(Bustles about the stage: the whole pantomime of senseless actions, common in their desperate nature: sniffs clothes, quickly leafs through a shut book, switches the lamp on and off, feels the glass in the window, and so on)* Tullius?! How . . . how come? And Ovid. Ovid and Horace. Fifteen minus two. Equals thirteen. Unlucky number. I always knew it. What? Knew what? Numbers were abolished. Gone. Why numbers? What about them? What've they got to do with it? Numbers! . . . Tullius gone! Missed such a day! What shall I . . . Who shall I . . . Oh, I shall go out of my mind! . . . What have you left me for, bastaaaaaaard? Who hast *(falls on his knees)* thou forsaken me for, ah? *(Opens his mouth wide)* Ah? Ah? Ah? Here it is, here it is . . . Coming to get me . . . T-i-i-i-ime *(Retreats—eyes filled with horror—backstage)* For there's nothing anymooooooore . . . *(Pause, now in a calm tone)* On the other hand, they must send a replacement. A sacred spot's never empty. And it'd be better if somebody young and fresh . . . *(A quick glance at the mirror, pulls his stomach in)* . . . They're bound to send someone! Can't do otherwise. Regardless of the Senate liberals. 'Cause the space can't be wasted. No sir. Eight square meters per nose! That's what the law says. And what would I do with all this space? Ah? An extra bed . . . A cup, too . . . as well as a toga . . . Tullius! What am I to do with this, ah? This is what it will look like when I, too . . . when I as well . . . "Whether they were true or bogus/All they've left behind is togas" . . . Main thing—a spare cup. Spare and empty . . . Tullius! . . . Wait . . . Maybe they were just putting this on . . . On tape, of course . . . Stereoscopic, three-dimensional . . . was in the papers: just invented. That's why he doesn't reply. Naturally. Because—on tape . . . *(Suddenly grabs his still-steaming coffeepot and rushes across the stage to* TULLIUS's *alcove, seizes* TULLIUS's *empty cup, pours coffee into it, and drinks)* Or—or—or else it's *me* they are showing to *him!* Live, of course. That's why he doesn't reply. Stop! That can't be! *(Seizes his temples)* Or—or—or else this . . . is a superimposition . . . Double exposure! Mixing the tapes! Or—tapes with live! Which is, after all, what life is all about! Reality, that is. Makes you want to look better, less paunchy . . . But then . . . what's the screen for, then?! *(Pours coffee into his own cup; drinks)* Or else—this is the tape being played to "live." Which is the definition of reality. Its full formula . . . In any case, how the devil did he do it? *(Opens the lid of the chute, looks down)* Tulliuuuuus, hey hey he—e—e—y! . . . In any case, if there is a replacement, the younger the better . . . Even if it's just a tape . . . And the sooner the better . . . *(Picks up the telephone and dials the number)* Mr. Praetor, sir. This is Publius Marcellus in 1750 . . . Yes, good morning, Mr. Praetor. Tullius Varro has vanished. Yes, I can't find him. I suppose he's escaped. And I wonder . . . What? You—what? You know? B-b-b-but how? The cameras, was it? I mean, cameras, Mr. Praetor. Live from the cell . . . Sure, sure, "nothing of the sort"? And you expect me to believe you? Wha-a-a-t? He rang you himself? And you expect me . . . From where? From what street? What, via dei Funari?! . . . But that's . . . that's only a stone's throw from the capitol! . . . Mr. Praetor, that man's dangerous . . . Ah? What? He asked to pass on that he'd bought some millet? Millet? *(Shouts)* What millet?! What millet, Mr. Praetor?! Are you out of your gourd? What? For the canary? Holy Jupiter! Where? Where you said? An establishment called Selva? What, two kilos? He's sorry it's only two kilos? That he had only half a sesterce? A-a-a-a-ah! *(Clutches his head)* On his way where? . . . Home?? . . . Mr. Praetor, what do you mean? . . . What? . . . Returning home? He is returning home? He is coming back?! . . . Mr. Prae— . . . What do you mean, calm down? . . . What do you . . . Yes. Yes, Mr. Praetor, sir . . . Yes, got them . . . tranclivi . . . trankviri . . . tranqu-ill-izers- tranquillizers . . . Yes, take two . . . But he's still . . . What? In five minutes? . . . If not sooner? Immediately after disinfection? . . . What? Yes, wash them down with water . . . *(Hangs up)* Oh my, oh my, oh my, oh my . . . What is going on, birds and animals *(Unconsciously rubs his palm along the keyboard: name—number—request: tranquillizers flash up; then a tray with pills and a glass of water appear from the opening)* On the other hand, they could have shoved some old bum in here. No guarantees, are there? . . . The same law for everyone . . . Although it might have been a boy . . . For the same reason . . . (Jumps up, suddenly realizing something)* My sleeping pills! *(Grabs the bottle and starts to bustle feverishly about the cell, looking for a place to hide it)* He'll find them . . . and here, too . . . and here . . . in the books? . . . no . . . Eureka! *(Rushes to* TULLIUS's *alcove and conceals the bottle under the bed. It is in this position—on his knees—that* TULLIUS *finds him as he steps from the elevator door)*

TULLIUS: What are you scrabbling for under there?

PUBLIUS: Oh, it's you. *(With an assumed calm)* My sandal. I've lost it.

T U L L I U S : Left or right?

P U B L I U S : Right. Although in principle they are alike.

T U L L I U S : Like the feet themselves. Like the feet . . .

P U B L I U S : Had breakfast?

T U L L I U S : Yes, with the Praetor. Though I wouldn't say no to coffee. *(Notices dregs in his cup)* What's this! Who's been drinking from my cup?

P U B L I U S : I thought . . .

T U L L I U S : Getting too brazen, you rascal. And so quickly . . . I hope you've slept in your own bed, did you . . . Barbarian is the word . . .

P U B L I U S : I thought you weren't coming back . . .

T U L L I U S : Well, what if I hadn't! What d'you need two cups for? Shitting the place up, eh? Got homesick for the mud, did you? *Nostalgie de la boue.* Ancestral calling. The Eastern bazaar. Shit-horseflies. *(Rinses the cup in the washbasin)* Microbes.

P U B L I U S : Racist . . . I thought you wouldn't be back and, well, you know, and got—what's the word?—nostalgic. And well, I thought, let me drink from his cup . . . Who knows, I thought, it might still smell of Tullius . . .

T U L L I U S : Oh yeah? And what is it that Tullius smells of?

P U B L I U S *(Exploding)*: Piss! Sewers and piss! Shit! What did you come back for, eh?! For you got away, didn't you! Got the hell out of here! Why, why, why, why the flaming hell did you have to come back?!

T U L L I U S : Now, how about the sleeping pills?

P U B L I U S : Sleeping pills—what?

T U L L I U S : We had a bet.

P U B L I U S : And?

T U L L I U S : And you lost.

P U B L I U S : And?

T U L L I U S : That's why I came back: (a) To prove that you'd lost. (b) For the pills.

PUBLIUS: You're out of your mind! You're out of your mind! How could you?! You got away! And from the Tower, of all places! You were free! Could have gone anywhere! And—and—and *(lost for words)* and—you'll swap freedom for sleeping pills!

TULLIUS: Hasn't it ever crossed your mind, dear Publius, hasn't it ever crossed your mind—or whatever you have instead—that sleeping pills *are* freedom. And, of course, vice versa . . .

PUBLIUS: Oh, go to . . . with all your paradoxes! . . . You got away! You found out how to! And you didn't tell me, you sod.

TULLIUS: Well, you wouldn't have confided in me either—had you been in my place . . .

PUBLIUS: True; but I wouldn't have come back, mind you! Which would have meant that a way to escape did exist! While you—you've reduced the chances! One less way to escape. Maybe the last one. It did exist! And now doesn't.

TULLIUS: A way to escape, Publius, is always there . . . Whereas a way of staying . . . Escape—what do you think escape proves? That the system's imperfect. Which, of course, suits you fine. As you, Publius, are what?—a barbarian. And therefore, for you, the Praetor is an enemy, the Tower is a dungeon. And so forth. For me, he's nobody, the Tower's nothing. And they—nobody and nothing—should be perfect. Otherwise, why not go back to barracks and barbed wire?

PUBLIUS: Sure; a bit more cheerful, at any rate.

TULLIUS: Sooner or later, everything becomes an object of nostalgia. That's why elegies are the most popular genre.

PUBLIUS: And epitaphs.

TULLIUS: Yes. Unlike utopias. Speaking of which, where are my sleeping pills?

PUBLIUS: Could be anywhere. Because—you've come back. By yourself, of course; but that's the same as being caught. It doesn't matter how. With their bare hands or with an idea. Ideas, frankly, are the best bloodhounds there are.

TULLIUS: Still, even so: we had a bet. And you lost. I won. For it's all about winning, right? And it's the winning . . . It's the winning I came back for. *(Enunciating every syllable)* Where—are—my—sleeping—pills?

PUBLIUS: How do I know! Out there, you could have tons of them. Unlimited. And for free. As decreed by the Senate. Freedom means sleeping pills. Your own words. Gratis and unlimited. Just stretch a hand . . . And you . . .

TULLIUS: The issue wasn't just sleeping pills.

PUBLIUS: But?

TULLIUS: But *your* sleeping pills.

PUBLIUS *(Shudders)*: You mean, my freedom?

(Pause)

TULLIUS: Let's forget high-flown words, Publius. Now, where's the bottle?

PUBLIUS: Where my right sandal is. Under your bed.

TULLIUS: Hmmm. Clever. *(Looks at* PUBLIUS *with interest)* I wouldn't have guessed that . . . not in my life. *(Produces the bottle from under the bed and hides it in the folds of his toga)* I'm going to get changed. I'm soaked through. It's raining pitchforks.

PUBLIUS *(A quick glance at the window: bright, shining noonday)*: But it's summer now, isn't it?

TULLIUS *(From behind a partition)*: In Rome, Publius, it's always summer. Even in winter.

PUBLIUS *(Another glance at the window)*: At least it's morning now, eh? About ten, as the Christians say . . .

TULLIUS: Morning, morning. Don't get worried. They haven't learned to control that yet . . .

PUBLIUS: Not in their interests. Reducing the day's length, I mean.

TULLIUS: Well, why's that?

P U B L I U S : 'Cause it's for life. Nor is it in their interest to extend it either.

T U L L I U S *(Pensively)*: Nn-yes . . . A threat of an epic there. No more, no less. *(Appears from behind the partition, clad in a freshly pressed toga; walks over to the table, pours himself some coffee, produces a cigar from the depths of his toga, and lounges comfortably on a couch. The first ring of smoke)*

P U B L I U S : So, no bean spilling, then, huh?

T U L L I U S : What?

P U B L I U S : I mean . . . about how you managed . . . to pull it off, that is. About the plan and all that, huh? 'Cause it doesn't matter anymore, you see. Now, that is. *Post factum.*

T U L L I U S : You wouldn't share your pills with me either; even *post factum.*

P U B L I U S : Why, what have the pills got to do with it?! You could have grabbed them all while I was asleep.

T U L L I U S *(Clearly and emphatically)*: I am not a thief, Publius. I am not a thief. Even you won't make a thief out of me. I am a Roman, and Romans don't steal. I earned that bottle. Got it? Earned. With my bent back. Literally at that.

P U B L I U S : Big deal, "bent back." Just shooed the classics into the shaft. The Christians used to do that, too.

T U L L I U S : Yes, but for them it was easier. In the first place, the shafts were shafts. At least they were spared worrying whether a shaft was real or just a tape. Secondly, I didn't just throw them down the shaft; I followed them myself.

P U B L I U S : That's what the classics are for: imitation. The lords of the mind, right? In short, you're both your own martyr and your own torturer. And all that over a handful of stinking pills.

T U L L I U S : Curiously enough *(turning the bottle in his fingers)*, it was precisely this flask that suggested the whole idea.

P U B L I U S : How do you mean? *(Leaps to his feet)*

T U L L I U S : It's just that it is a cylinder, and the shaft is a cylinder. Only longer. And not so transparent. Narrow as well, though. Less than a meter in diameter. About 75 centimeters, at best. And the walls are too slippery.

PUBLIUS: Greased, you mean?

TULLIUS: That, and because it's damp as well. And moldy in places.

PUBLIUS: And?

TULLIUS: And so I decided not to go feet first like a dummy but to stuff in my mattress, folded in half. It, the mattress, that is, would try to unbend; that is, it'd get stuck there, press against the sides, there'd be friction. Which might not happen if you went down feet first. Like a dummy.

PUBLIUS: That's for sure . . .

TULLIUS: So we rode down this way, together . . . As soon as you get acceleration, you just press the mattress to the shaft side. With your feet . . . It's like braking.

PUBLIUS: Did it take long?

TULLIUS: About as long as a bowel movement. Or as a shower. Though it smelled like a bowel movement. It was dark, too.

PUBLIUS: And then?

TULLIUS: Then the shredder, smashed by the classics. Then the cloaca: formerly catacombs. Then it delivers you to the Tiber . . . And then I swam.

PUBLIUS: When our cohort was stationed at Leptis Magna . . .

TULLIUS: Publius, I beg you . . .

PUBLIUS: No, it's just that I got a laurel wreath for swimming . . . Oh well, never mind . . . *(Waves his hand)* Now I guess they'll go and set up a worse chopper than ever. Electronic one. Or lasers. The last word of . . .

TULLIUS: Aha, pulverizers. Elementary particles . . . On the other hand, they have reasons. We're not the only ones here. There's the restaurant, after all. Plus TV antennae. Other cells. Perhaps even antiaircraft batteries. Can you imagine how much garbage it all makes?

P U B L I U S: Where do you think the kitchen is? Above or below us?

T U L L I U S: Above probably. Since products are bound to end up below, anyway. This way they have a chance to get up. To glance at the world, if you will.

P U B L I U S *(Miserably)*: The best way to look at the world is close up. The closer you are, the sharper your senses become . . .

T U L L I U S: The sense of smell only . . . If you're so homesick for the world, I won't flush the john after myself.

P U B L I U S: Very witty. Do you think that makes a difference? After you, that is? . . . These, by the way *(With sudden hope in his voice jabbing his finger at the two remaining busts)* . . . What did you keep them for?

T U L L I U S *(Shaking his head)*: No, not for that . . . Just for breeding, for cultivation . . . Great personal attachment. I've loved Ovid since childhood. D'you know how *The Metamorphoses* ends? *(Recites)*

> Now I have finished my work, and neither Jupiter's anger
> will destroy it, nor steel, nor flames, nor Time's
> omniverous mouth . . .

then there's some la-di-da about him living on stars, and after:

> Everywhere on the earth where Rome stretches its power
> I'll be read by the people, and for ages and ages (if bards'
> forecasts are worth anything) I'll be nurtured by glory.

P U B L I U S: Never could stand hexameters.

T U L L I U S *(Continuing)*: Notice that stipulation—about forecasts. Bards' forecasts, at that. Inklings and premonitions . . . The guy, you see, is about to get carried away: this is for ages to come and all that . . . And yet, bang, he stops and chops off, so to speak, the very twig he's chirping from: "if bards' forecasts are worth anything" . . . and only then about "glory." Sobriety indeed . . .

PUBLIUS (*Despairingly*): Ah, what has that got to do with it! . . . Forecasts, premonitions . . . And they're installing a new chopper meanwhile . . . Now, that's a premonition . . .

TULLIUS: It's just that he turned out to be right. About the ages to come and about that glory. And why? Because he was doubtful. This bit about whether bards' inklings are worth anything—it came from doubt. He, too, had nothing ahead except "ages and ages." Except time, that is. He, too, had found himself at the edge of space—when your kid's namesake, Octavian Augustus, chased him out of Rome. Only he got to the horizontal edge of it; ours is the vertical one: . . . "Everywhere on earth where Rome stretches its power . . ." True, very true: stretches. To nearly a thousand meters above sea level at that. And two thousand years later. And if we are to multiply these . . . Still, he didn't foresee being read in rarefied air.

PUBLIUS: Very classy indeed.

TULLIUS: You're an ass, Publius; not a barbarian, but an ass. More precisely, a barbarian *and* his ass. As the poet said. About another poet . . . A classic, Publius, becomes a classic because of time. Not the time that passes after his death but the time while he's alive—it's all the same to him. And it's all the same for him, mind you, while he's alive. Because a poet always deals with time, one way or another. Whether he's young or decrepit. Even while scribbling about space. Because what is a song anyway but restructured time? Any song is. Even birdies' . . . Because a sound or, say, a note—it takes up a second, and the next one, too, takes up a second. Sounds, you know, they are different, while seconds, they're always the same. But because of the sounds, Publius, because of the sounds, the seconds, too, become different. Ask your canary, if you're on speaking terms. What d'you think it's chirping about? About time. And when it doesn't, that's about time also.

PUBLIUS: I thought it was about grub. That is, it sings when it hopes. And stops when it quits.

TULLIUS: Incidentally, I got some millet for it. Two kilos only. I had no more money.

PUBLIUS: I know. You bought it on via dei Funari.

TULLIUS: Aha, in Selva. How did you know?

PUBLIUS: The Praetor told me . . . It's where that stela with *memento mori* on it is, right?

TULLIUS: Aha. I knew a hetaera there once. Absolutely delightful creature. A brunette, eyes like fuzzy bumblebees. She kept her own peacocks. Could read and write also, knew the Emperor of China. It was her procurator—whom she in due course married—who set up Selva. So that she'd sell bird food and stay respectable. He was a swine, all right; chased me with a sword around the entire Forum.

PUBLIUS: It sounds quite elegiac.

TULLIUS: Just too many verbs in the past tense.

(Pause)

TULLIUS: Shall we fence a bit?

PUBLIUS: As early as this?

TULLIUS: Precisely. To limber up a bit. Get the blood moving. As the girl said to the legionary . . . Weighed yourself today?

PUBLIUS: Not yet. Yesterday. Same old story: I'm putting it on. Why is it, I wonder, so much easier to gain than to lose. Theoretically, it should be just as simple. Or just as hard. *(Gets up and walks to the keyboard)* Swords or daggers?

TULLIUS: Swords. Because of your mouth. Your breath, that is.

PUBLIUS: Mine just smells . . . Yours drops it out . . . Parthian or Greek?

TULLIUS: Greek.

PUBLIUS *(Pressing a button on the keyboard, where the text of his request flashes up: Greek swords)*: Still, what is it that nature's trying to say by that? That increasing in size is more natural than getting smaller? *(The swords appear;* P U B L I U S *and* T U L L I U S *sort them out, continuing to talk)* And what are the limits? That is, on the one hand, when you grow up, from a boy into a man, you are increasing. Over, say, twenty to thirty years. And that creates inertia. But why precisely your belly? Is it because you move forward? . . . On the other hand, where are you moving to? It's clear where. Where you won't need a paunch. Nor its absence. In the next world. So-called.

T U L L I U S *(Trying the sword in his hand)*: Who knows, the greater the size, the longer you can linger in this world. So-called. At least you'll rot longer. Decomposition, Publius, is also a form of presence.

P U B L I U S: Sure; if you're not cremated, of course . . . Up to the Praetor, though . . . Well, shall we start? . . . *En garde!* Till first blood.

T U L L I U S: Till first blood.

(They fence)

P U B L I U S: But if getting bigger *(thrust)* is natural, then getting smaller *(retreat)* is artificial.

T U L L I U S: And what's wrong with being artificial? *(Thrust)* Everything artificial is *(another thrust)* natural. More precisely, the artificial starts where the natural *(retreat)* ends.

P U B L I U S: And where does *(thrust)* the artificial end?

T U L L I U S: What's really horrible, Publius *(counterthrust)*, is that the artificial ends nowhere. The natural comes to an end naturally. *(Pushes* P U B L I U S *toward his alcove)* That is, it becomes artificial. While the artificial never ends. *(Thrust)* Nowhere. *(Another thrust)* Never. *(Yet another thrust)* Under any guise. *(*P U B L I U S *falls into his alcove)* Because after it nothing follows. And this, as the poet has it,

This is worse than the word said
to soothe children after a fall,
because after this there follows
nothing at all.

P U B L I U S: What poet?

T U L L I U S: A Scythian.

P U B L I U S *(Resting)*: Maybe the artificial if it keeps being artificial long enough becomes natural. Since the egg does become
the chicken. Though looking from the outside, you wouldn't
guess it. And it doesn't look promising from the inside either.
Just white and artificial. I always had a feeling looking at an
egg, in the morning, especially when you break it to make an
omelette, that there was once a civilization which learned to
produce canned goods organically.

T U L L I U S: In that sense we're all canned goods. Someone's
future omelette. Unless, of course, they cremate us. Pick up
your sword.

P U B L I U S *(Unwillingly climbs out of his alcove)*: I've got too
heavy . . . Now, in Libya I remember . . . *(Suddenly with irritation)* Ah, what's the point of staying in shape! Getting slim?
Spoiling someone's omelette . . . Especially if cremated! Besides,
it's to your advantage: the fatter I get, the more space I take
up . . . And so the more of that time of yours you're left with . . .
For it's all the same for everybody, beginning with you,
whether Publius Marcellus exists or doesn't! And even if he
does, who cares about the way he looks. Who's interested in
that? The gods? Caesar? Nature? Who? . . . The gods don't give
a damn. Neither does Caesar. In this sense, he's their anointed
indeed. Nature? Does nature care for the silhouette of a tree?

T U L L I U S: Sounds like a topic for some arty symposium.

P U B L I U S: I don't think nature gives a shit about a tree's silhouette. Even though . . . changes . . . four times a year. But
that's precisely a sign of indifference. Satiety! Tearing the

little leaves off . . . While maybe all that tree ever had in this world was just those little leaves . . . Maybe all it wanted to do on this earth was just to count them one by one . . . its little green money . . . its small golden change . . . And—whoosh! . . .

TULLIUS: Oh, sniveling again. Pick up your sword, I said . . . And anyway, there are evergreens as well. Laurels, say. Conifers. And so forth.

PUBLIUS: All right, let's say I pick up the sword. Then what? We'll cross them. Then we'll back off. Thrust, counterthrust, withdraw. Then what? We get tired. Then what? You'll win, I'll lose. Or vice versa. Who cares? Who's going to see this duel? Even if I kill you—or vice versa. Although we agreed. Till first blood. But who's to see that? Who wants to watch such rubbish? Especially live. Even the Praetor won't. The Praetor will see it on tape and, if there's no murder, might just as well erase it. At the end of the working day. And not because he'd begrudge the tape or because the spools need greasing; no—because there's no subject.

TULLIUS: Wrong. They tape everything, without selecting. They're not allowed to erase by law. Who knows, the style of some criminal can be picked up. Even though no crime has been committed. A style all the same. Of a possible criminal. In order to solve a possible crime. Which is the formula for reality. So there is a subject, Publius. A subject always emerges, in spite of the author. Moreover, in spite of the characters. Of actors as well. And of the public. Because the real audience is not them. Neither the stalls nor the gallery. They, too, are actors. Or rather, non-actors. We have only one spectator—time. So let's do some fencing.

PUBLIUS (*Reluctantly picks up his sword*): Well, from this spectator you don't get much applause, ever. Even if you win. Not to mention if you lose. *En garde.*

(*They fence*)

T U L L I U S : Because winning is *(thrust)* melodrama and losing *(another thrust)* is melodrama. *(Retreating under* P U B L I U S*'s attack)* Escape is melodrama, so is suicide. Time, Publius, is a great stylist . . . *(Attacks)*

P U B L I U S *(Defending himself)*: Then what *(parries)* isn't melodrama?

T U L L I U S : Well, this. *(Thrust)* Fencing. *(Falls back)* This movement: back and forth, across the stage. Like a pendulum. Anything . . . that doesn't raise the tone . . . or the pitch . . . Anything . . . that doesn't imitate life . . . but goes tick-tock . . . Anything that's monotonous . . . that doesn't crow like a cockerel . . . The more monotonous, the more it's like truth.

P U B L I U S *(Dropping the sword)*: Touché; but one can flail this way till the end of the world.

T U L L I U S *(Continuing to make automatic revolutions with his sword)*: And during it. And after. And after-after-after-after . . . Till first blood. Or second. Or to-the-last-drop-of-blood . . . That's. Why. People. Fight . . . Ooooooof . . . Haven't we agreed: till the first . . . ?

P U B L I U S : You've cut my knee.

T U L L I U S : Oh . . . sorry. I didn't notice. Not serious, I hope.

P U B L I U S : It's nothing. A scratch. As the lion said to the gladiator.

T U L L I U S : There's cotton and iodine in the medicine chest. Bandage it. I'm going to take a shower. I'm all sweaty . . . *(Disappears into the shower)*

P U B L I U S *(Thoughtfully)*: No-o-o. Let it run. At least it proves I'm not a statue yet. Nor marble. Not a classic. Because here is a knee. Fairly classical, in its own way. Not any worse than in *Vigil of Alcibiades*. Although I've seen only a copy. Or in the *Discus Thrower*. Also a copy. And the knee's not the main thing there . . . All the same, it's classical. With such a knee, governors crush local princelings. On the wet floor of a marble bathhouse. At their suburban villa. A lilac-tinted evening . . .

Torches quiver in niches, oil melts . . . Palm crowns whisper with one another like live Chinese characters . . . And the princeling, bastard, is writhing on the wet floor, gasping for air with his open mouth . . . No-o, it's a good knee. Roman. Whatever Tullius may spill on that tape . . . Let it drip. Let it. And I'll even open it up a bit more . . . *(Takes the sword and, grimacing, cuts the skin; after that, he squeezes blood from the cut with his fingers; he is caught at this by* T U L L I U S *who emerges from the shower, watches the scene for a while, then takes a step toward* P U B L I U S*)*

T U L L I U S : What are you doing?! Gone completely nuts! Stop it at once! Blasted barbarian! Savage. Where's the cotton?

P U B L I U S *(Lifting his eyes: there are tears in them)*: You look nice 'n' clean, Tullius . . .

T U L L I U S : You half-baked idiot! *(Rushes to the medicine chest, gets iodine and cotton, and rushes back)* You've remembered your Asiatic tricks, have you? No matter how much one feeds a wolf . . . *(Bends over* P U B L I U S *to bandage the knee)* People are landing on Canopus, but here . . .

P U B L I U S *(Brushes him away)*: Leave me alone! Don't touch it . . .

T U L L I U S : I see. Now we'll fall into a trance. We'll start rocking, to and fro. We'll draw a sign on our forehead. And sing something devoid of text. Right? *(Bends over* P U B L I U S *again)* Give me your leg and stop playing the idiot . . .

P U B L I U S : Go away, I told you. *(Makes a threatening gesture with his sword)* Leave me alone. Don't touch it. Let it drip . . .

T U L L I U S : Now stop this crap, will you . . .

P U B L I U S : Let it drip. Maybe it's the only proof left . . . that I'm really alive . . . And you want to stop it. Who are you working for?

T U L L I U S *(Taken aback)*: You . . . I think . . . you've gone mad.

P U B L I U S : It's these cameras all around. One starts suspecting everybody. How do I know that you're not a robot. With a built-in camera. Inserted organically. Maybe even against your will. They started that a while back, under, I think, Tiberius. On rabbits, I've heard . . . And besides, you came back. That's when they inserted it . . . Quite likely . . . No, let it drip. At least, I'll know that *I'm* not a robot. For I was starting to have my doubts . . . For maybe everything—*everything*—you included—is a tape. And it's shown to me. Stereoscopically. Including smells. Like swans and gardens. Or that seashore. And that's why this backdrop is always the same: because their budget is limited. Or because of classicism. Because they observe the three unities. And why not. If it's a choice between naturalism and classicism, I'd choose classicism myself. And why shouldn't the computer be snobbish? Snobbery, you know, is also a form of despair. After all, despair's got classicism programmed into it. It didn't just drop from the ceiling. And speaking of the ceiling, Tullius, it, too, came to that—that I am looking up, and I don't know any longer whether it's me looking at it or . . . or vice versa.

TULLIUS: What kind of garbage is that?

PUBLIUS: The whole point is who you are working for . . . That I am looking at it, well, this is obvious even to a hedgehog. That it looks at me . . . But if yes . . . if it's carrying out surveillance on me, then it pays more attention to me than I do to it. And then, which one is the more alive? . . . And of course if you are not a robot, its attention gets split . . . No, let it drip, this sort of thing hasn't been seen by it yet . . . A bit of novelty for it . . .

TULLIUS: Bandage it up, I tell you. It's disgusting!

PUBLIUS: Therefore—you're not a robot . . . On the other hand, I, too, would have been scared of a crack in the ceiling . . . A crack, you see, couldn't have been taped. It's only the possibility of a catastrophe that distinguishes reality from fiction.

TULLIUS: Melodrama. All barbarians have an innate feeling for melodrama.

PUBLIUS *(Shouts)*: I must know the place I am going to die in, mustn't I!

TULLIUS: A-a-ah, so that's what it is. *(Throws cotton and bandages to* PUBLIUS*)* Go on, tie it up. *(Walks away to the window; begins speaking while looking at it, but then recollects himself and turns first with his face to the audience, then with his back. While standing with his back to the audience, he is, as it were, leaning against an imaginary wall formed by the footlights)* People, Publius, are divided into those for whom it's important *where* and those for whom it's important *when* . . . There is, of course, a third category. Those for whom it matters *how*. But these as a rule are the young, and they don't count.

PUBLIUS: Just who do you think you are?! How do you know what people are divided into?

TULLIUS: Just these two categories. The process itself fixes the options. Reduces the choice, so to speak. And there are only two.

PUBLIUS: Oh sure. And I, of course, made the wrong choice. Goofed. And besides, why bother: if it's for life, then where else but in these four . . . πr . . . In this . . . what do you call it?

TULLIUS: πr^2?

PUBLIUS: Yeah, yeah . . . In πr square, in tender care . . . In fullest view . . . As they say in Scythia, in public even death is pretty . . . The worst pornography there is . . . I mean, to show *that* . . . That, and delivery . . . Because that's never *you* there. Even when you later watch your own delivery. On tape. All the same, that's not you.

TULLIUS *(Gets the legal codex from the shelf)*: Let's see . . . Letter *P* . . . yes . . . "Pornography: any inanimate object provoking an erection . . ." That's what Tiberius says on the subject.

P U B L I U S *(Exploding)*: Why do you keep ramming that cretin down my throat all the time! Tiberius this, Tiberius that! Just like the Christians with their . . . what's his name?—ah, who cares . . . he only lasted for thirty-three years . . . What could he know? Especially for the rest of us pushing forty . . . Pushing fifty . . . That's what did them in, by the way . . . Tiberius! Inanimate object! Erection! . . . The biggest erection is when it's not you who's dying . . .

T U L L I U S : Nn-yes . . . If I were the last man on earth . . .

P U B L I U S : . . . you'd have a hard-on like this Tower . . . On the other hand, why deny thy neighbor a pleasure. Let them tape it. Or put it out live. Maybe I'll manage some clever last words . . . After all, Tullius, I have nothing against all this *(a broad sweep of the arm)* πr square. Of course, claustrophobia at times flares up when it dawns on you that it's precisely right here . . . So you want to escape from here not as from a place of life but as from a place of death . . . That is, I'm not against it, Tullius, don't get me wrong. And neither am I *against* the Tower and *for* freedom . . . I think freedom is better than the Tower . . . well, maybe . . . I don't remember it any longer . . . Still, freedom is a variation on the theme of death. On the theme of where it's going to happen. In other words, on the theme of the coffin . . . Whereas here—well, here the coffin . . . well, it's right here . . . The only thing that's unclear is—when. *Where* is clear. It's precisely the clarity that scares me, Tullius. Others are scared of the unknown. Me, of the known.

T U L L I U S : But really, there's nothing wrong with this place. Well, perhaps they've overdone it a bit with hidden cameras. But that's only to make it more like the world outside. Besides, who knows: maybe you're right. Maybe they really are just showing us all this. And most likely, a tape. It could well be that all this is but convention. Requirement of a genre. Had it been a reality, it wouldn't arouse so much emotion.

P U B L I U S : It's here I'll die, reality or not . . .

T U L L I U S : Well, that's the drawback of space, Publius. The main drawback, I should say . . . That it contains a spot in which we'll cease to be . . . That's why, I suppose, they pay so much attention to it.

P U B L I U S : Yeah, but time has such a place also. Plenty of such places . . .

T U L L I U S *(Didactically)*: Time, Publius, has everything except place. Especially since they abolished numbers . . . While space . . . any point in it can become . . . That's why they are so keen on depicting it. All these landscapes and country scenes. Sketches from nature. Pure subconscious . . . With time, tricks like that won't do . . . Well, perhaps some portrait . . . or a still life . . .

P U B L I U S : And it's all the same to you where. Right?

T U L L I U S : It's all the same to me where, and it's all the same when.

P U B L I U S : Of course, of course! Roman virtues! Patrician restraint! Mucius Scaevola! Baked hands! If you're not interested in where or when, what, then, are you interested in? *How?*

T U L L I U S : Close, Publius, but no cigar. What interests me is not "how" but "how many"?

P U B L I U S : How many what?

T U L L I U S : How many hours of staying awake represent the minimum required by the computer to define one's condition as *being*. That is, that I am alive. And how many pills am I supposed to take at one swallow to guarantee that minimum.

P U B L I U S : Eh? I don't get it.

T U L L I U S : Please don't get me wrong. It's not that I'm sick of talking to you. Though partly I am. Nor is it because I haven't slept all night. Though that's also the case. It's simply that I really want to become more like time. To approximate its rhythm, that is. Since I'm not a poet and can't create a new one . . . The only thing I'd like to try is to make my existence a bit more monotonous; less melodramatic. More suited to the tastes of that spectator . . . Putting it crudely, to sleep more. Eight hours asleep, sixteen awake: that version of time I've already mastered. Perhaps one could rearrange it a bit.

P U B L I U S *(Stunned by all he has heard)*: How on earth do you mean!?

T U L L I U S : Say, sixteen hours of sleep and eight hours awake. Or eighteen and six. The less wakefulness, the more sleep— and the more interesting the version of time. Space, you see, Publius, is always the same—horizontal. Whereas time . . . You see, I've tried something already. Well, sleeping during the daytime and not sleeping at night. Or staying awake for three days in a row, and vice versa . . . But in the first place, in these circumstances *(nods toward the window)*, additional energy is expended on defining day and night. It's quite hard to deter- mine just how long a day is. Secondly—and this I must say disturbs me most of all—there is a certain minimum of wake- fulness after which—if I fail to observe it—the computer ceases to supply my food. And then I shall have to beg from you. Most likely, to trade food for sleeping pills. And that would spoil the whole idea. Not to mention that we would have entered into a kind of relationship unforeseen by Tiberius in design- ing the Tower and, probably, repugnant to us ourselves.

P U B L I U S *(Quickly)*: What do you mean by "repugnant"?

T U L L I U S : Well, barter, you know, theft, suspicions, denunci- ations to the Praetor . . . well, you've lived in Rome . . . and until I explained to the Praetor what it was all about and until he had agreed to believe my story . . .

P U B L I U S *(Getting up and limping toward the telephone)*: Perhaps we could ask the Praetor how many pills you need to take . . .

T U L L I U S : No, no, no way! *(Whispering with a finger to his lips)* I am not entitled to any more pills! I used up my quota last month. No, no one must know! It's a secret . . . After all, if a poet's interested in time professionally, I am just an amateur. And amateurs act intuitively . . . Well, you, for example, how many do you take a night?

PUBLIUS: Two, two and a half. Three.

TULLIUS: Let's work it out, then. Three pills equals eight hours' sleep. Sixteen hours, therefore, should equal six pills. Let's remember: sixteen equals six. That is, six to sixteen. Suppose we need seventeen hours. To get seventeen, the dose must be increased from six to—how many? Stop. Wait. Let's divide sixteen into six. That is, hours into pills. And the outcome is . . . Stop. Rubbish. Let's do it the other way around. Divide pills into hours. Six into sixteen. The outcome is . . . The outcome, in the first place, is a fraction. Are you following the train of thought, Publius?

PUBLIUS: With envy and admiration.

TULLIUS: Just wait, there's more to come. So, a fraction . . . plus . . . I've lost it. Anyway, even if we stick to round figures, we get *(with an effort, both he and* PUBLIUS *bend fingers, counting)* one pill equaling four hours of sleep. So if we want to keep squashing the bedbugs for seventeen hours, we'd need . . . we'd need . . . about seven . . . seven and a bit . . . *(Uncertainly)* Is that right . . . We'd need . . .

PUBLIUS: We've got all we need! . . . Time-shmime . . . Isn't a life term long enough for you? . . . What are you trying . . .

TULLIUS: The whole point, dear Tullius, is that a life term has a knack for turning into a death term. Which means that your posthumous situation is a spin-off of your lifetime condition. Coming to terms, you know . . . Which means that during every lifetime one has a chance to find out what things are going to be like afterward . . . And a Roman must not miss such an opportunity.

PUBLIUS: Snooping is the word . . .

TULLIUS *(Shouts)*: It snoops on us, doesn't it?

P U B L I U S: Snooping, then. Peeping. Through a little hole . . .

T U L L I U S: Well, in a sense, yes. But without actually looking! With eyes closed. In a horizontal position.

P U B L I U S: When our cohort was stationed in Gaul . . .

T U L L I U S: Publius! I beg you! In the name of all that's . . .

P U B L I U S: . . . I knew a Greek. Terribly enterprising fellow. In real estate . . . And he had this building. Six or eight stories, I don't remember. Ordinary families lived there. You know, husband, wife, child. And do you know what the beast thought up? Instead of normal light bulbs, he screwed in some miniature TV cameras. So for three sesterces you could watch an hour of family life. Copulation, I mean. The whole kick was that they might not feel like doing it that day. And your sesterces go down the drain. Or else they did it . . .

T U L L I U S: What are you telling me this for?

P U B L I U S: What queues he had! Precisely because of the element of probability! You don't know how that sort of thing can set someone on fire! And especially if they had a baby . . . And they put him to bed first . . . Or he wakes up while they're at it . . . Oh my! . . . And she, all lathered up, unhitches herself and staggers off into the kid's room . . . And especially if she's a blonde . . . And then she gets back, and he is still holding his thing . . .

T U L L I U S: Shut up, I said!

P U B L I U S: He made a fortune, that Greek. Opened a whole chain afterward. Argus, the company was called. Haven't you heard the name?

T U L L I U S: Never.

P U B L I U S: That means you got the idea all on your own.

T U L L I U S *(Counting pills in the flask)*: In the good old days, Publius, people like you had their tongues pulled out, their ears cut off, and their eyes put out for buttons. Or else, they were flayed alive . . . Perhaps I put up with all this only because to punish someone who's already punished—first by this cell, secondly by the way your mind operates, would be tautological. A theater within a theater.

PUBLIUS: Or, for you, like stepping into dog shit . . . *(Places his palm on his belly)* Lunchtime's soon.

TULLIUS: I'm going to lie down. No sleep last night . . . *(Counts the pills)* Sleep, sleep . . . Don't grab my portion, will you . . . What have we got today? . . . Pigeon-liver pâté . . . and trout with stork's eggs . . . N-n-yes . . . Fish finally . . . At least leave me the eggs . . . for breakfast . . . Well, to make sure . . . To make sure, let's *(shakes out pills onto his palm)* take an even number . . . Let's take eight. *(Pours wine into a goblet, swallows the pills, and washes them down)*

PUBLIUS: Wait, don't go . . . Wait a minute . . . What am I . . . going to do? Sixteen hours in a row . . .

TULLIUS: Seventeen.

PUBLIUS: Even worse! Have you thought about me? Egoist! Patrician! You're all alike! That's why nobody likes you . . . What am *I* going to do? You don't give a shit about me, do you?

TULLIUS: Don't yell! . . . There's a stereo. Also, look at the TV. Books as well. Space programs too. On tape . . . Read the classics over there . . . It's best to read them when you know how they looked . . . Stroll around a bit . . . It's all yours . . .

PUBLIUS: Thanks a lot! Thanks a lot! Stroll! . . . And besides, my knee hurts! . . . And who on earth am I to talk to? . . . Seventeen hours! . . . I'll just . . . I'd go mad! . . . *(Screams)* I can't take iiiiit!

TULLIUS: What is there to take, what are you babbling about . . . *(Yawns)* On the contrary, I'm leaving you in peace . . . *(Yawns)* And when I wake up, I'll tell you everything I've seen . . . about time . . . They show you things there as well . . . you know *(Yawns)* . . .

PUBLIUS: Stop yawning! . . . *(Seizes* TULLIUS *by the hem of his toga)* Wait! . . . don't lie down yet . . . Wait! Oh, what can I . . . *(Clutches his head)* Alone . . . in this πr square . . . like a point encircled by a compass . . . What are you doing to me, bastard! . . . As though I am not a human being . . . My kneeeeeee hurts! . . . Stop yaaaaawning . . . Oh, my head is bursting! How can you? . . . Don't you see? . . .

T U L L I U S *(Yawning; almost naked)*: No, the gray one's better . . . It's more like time . . . Which . . . What's so special about a human being? . . . *(Yawns)* It's an exclamation mark . . . *(yawns)* that becomes a question mark . . . *(Starts to take off his toga)* That becomes a dash . . . *(Yawns)* Turn around . . .

P U B L I U S: Why?

T U L L I U S: So I can hide the pills. And get changed.

P U B L I U S *(Turns away)*: I wouldn't have taken them anyhow . . . don't be long.

T U L L I U S *(Yawns)*: Just a sec . . . just a sec . . . *(Hides the pills in the canary's cage)* A sec . . . just one more sec . . . *(Returns to the alcove)* Now, where is my toga? *(Yawns)* The woolly one? . . .

P U B L I U S *(Turns back)*: Better take the white one.

T U L L I U S: I asked you to turn around. I'm changing.

P U B L I U S: What's wrong with having an eyeful? . . . Why that one? Take the white one.

T U L L I U S *(Yawning; almost naked)*: No, the gray one's better . . . It's more like time . . . Which, Publius *(yawns)*, is of a gray color . . . Like the sky in the north . . . or maybe the waves . . . *(Yawns; unfurls the toga widely)* You see? Here's how time really looks . . . Or *(folds it in half)* like this . . . Or *(folds it otherwise)* like this . . . Just a gray cloth. *(Wraps himself in the toga and lies down)*

(Pause)

P U B L I U S: How can it be? How . . . I shan't know even how much time has passed! 'Cause they've abolished hourglasses as well. So much for those African colonies . . . How shall I know when . . .

T U L L I U S: Don't worry. I'll wake up myself. After seventeen hours. *(Yawns)* It will mean that seventeen hours have gone by when I wake up.

P U B L I U S: How can that be?

(Pause)

T U L L I U S: Publius.

P U B L I U S: Eh?

T U L L I U S: Do me a favor.

P U B L I U S: What?

T U L L I U S: Move Horace a bit closer.

(P U B L I U S moves the bust)

P U B L I U S: Like that?

T U L L I U S: Aha. Thank you. And Oooo *(yawns)*-vid.

P U B L I U S *(Moves the bust of Ovid)*: Like that?

T U L L I U S: Aha . . . a bit closer . . .

P U B L I U S: Like that?

T U L L I U S: A bit more . . .

P U B L I U S: Classics . . . A classic is closer to you than a simple man . . .

T U L L I U S *(Yawning)*: Than who?

P U B L I U S: Than a man.

T U L L I U S: A? . . . a man? A man, Publius . . . *(Yawns)* A man is as alone . . . *(yawns again)* . . . as a thought that's being forgotten.

CURTAIN